W9-AKW-711

Fire and Wind

Fire and Wind

The Holy Spirit
in the Church Today

Joseph D. Small
Editor

GENEVA

© 2002 by Joseph D. Small

All rights reserved. No part of this book may be reproduced or transmitted in any form or by any means, electronic or mechanical, including photocopying, recording, or by any information storage or retrieval system, without permission in writing from the publisher. For information, address Geneva Press, 100 Witherspoon Street, Louisville, Kentucky 40202-1396.

Scripture quotations from the New Revised Standard Version of the Bible are copyright © 1989 by the Division of Christian Education of the National Council of the Churches of Christ in the U.S.A., and are used by permission.

Scripture quotations from the Revised Standard Version of the Bible are copyright 1946, 1952, 1971, 1973 by the Division of Christian Education of the National Council of the Churches of Christ in the U.S.A. and are used by permission.

Scripture quotations marked NEB are taken from *The New English Bible,* © The Delegates of the Oxford University Press and The Syndics of the Cambridge University Press, 1961, 1970. Used by permission.

Excerpts from the Nicene Creed found in the Book of Confessions, 1999.

Book design by Sharon Adams
Cover design by Terry Dugan Design

First edition
Published by Geneva Press
Louisville, Kentucky

This book is printed on acid-free paper that meets the American National Standards Institute Z39.48 standard. ∞

PRINTED IN THE UNITED STATES OF AMERICA

02 03 04 05 06 07 08 09 10 11 — 10 9 8 7 6 5 4 3 2 1

Library of Congress Cataloging-in-Publication Data is on file at the Library of Congress, Washington, D.C.

ISBN 0-664-50172-9

For Valerie

. . . remembering before our God and Father
your work of faith
and labor of love
and steadfastness of hope in our Lord Jesus Christ

Contents

Contributors   ix

Introduction   xi

The Spirit and the Creed
    Joseph D. Small   1

We Believe in . . .   **19**

. . . The Holy Spirit, Who with the Father
and the Son Is Worshiped and Glorified
    Colin Gunton   21

. . . The Holy Spirit, Who Has Spoken
through the Prophets
    Cynthia M. Campbell   37

. . . One Holy Catholic and Apostolic Church
    Miroslav Volf   48

. . . One Baptism for the Forgiveness of Sins
    Leanne Van Dyk   65

Contemporary Issues   **77**

Why the Holy Spirit Now?
    Gregory Anderson Love   79

Holy Spirit and Human Spirit
    Willie James Jennings   89

The Trinity and the Christian Life
    Ellen T. Charry   106

The Holy Spirit and Spiritual Formation
    Elizabeth Nordquist   120

Proclamation   **133**
It's Not about You
    M. Craig Barnes   135
Doves, Deserts, and Bathtubs
    Linda C. Loving   140
God-Breath
    Nancy Copeland-Payton   146
Who Has the Spirit?
    Gregory M. Busby   152

Contributors

M. Craig Barnes is pastor of National Presbyterian Church, Washington, D.C.

Gregory M. Busby is pastor of First United Presbyterian Church, Charlotte, North Carolina

Cynthia Campbell is president and Cyrus McCormick Professor of Church and Ministry at McCormick Theological Seminary

Ellen T. Charry is Margaret W. Harmon Associate Professor of Systematic Theology at Princeton Theological Seminary

Nancy Copeland-Payton is pastor of First Presbyterian Church, Sand Point, Idaho

Colin Gunton is Professor of Christian Doctrine at King's College, University of London

Willie James Jennings is associate dean for academic programs and Assistant Research Professor at Duke Divinity School

Gregory Anderson Love is Assistant Professor of Systematic Theology at San Francisco Theological Seminary

Linda Loving is pastor of House of Hope Presbyterian Church, St. Paul, Minnesota

Elizabeth Nordquist is Assistant Professor of Spirituality at San Francisco Theological Seminary

Joseph D. Small is director of the Office of Theology and Worship, Presbyterian Church (U.S.A.)

Leanne Van Dyk is Professor of Reformed Theology at Western Theological Seminary

Miroslav Volf is Henry B. Wright Professor of Systematic Theology at Yale University Divinity School

Introduction

Almost twenty years ago, at the culmination of the well-known "Baptism, Eucharist, and Ministry" process, the Faith and Order Commission of the World Council of Churches initiated a new theological program, "Towards a Common Expression of the Apostolic Faith Today." This effort is central to the Council's function: calling the churches to "the goal of visible unity in one faith and one eucharistic fellowship." The ecumenical hope of visible unity lies neither in institutional consolidation nor vague togetherness, but is grounded in a living hope that has three essential conditions and elements:

- common confession of the apostolic faith
- mutual recognition of Baptism, Eucharist, and ministry
- common structures for witness, service, decision making, and teaching

"Towards a Common Expression of the Apostolic Faith Today" has proceeded with special attention to the Nicene Creed, although it is understood that "apostolic faith" is more broadly attested in the scriptures and summarized in the whole creedal tradition of the church's first five centuries. The great ecumenical creed of Nicaea and

Constantinople (325/381) occupies a special place within the creedal tradition, however, and is an appropriate focus for churches' efforts to reappropriate their common basis in the apostolic faith, to join in common confession of faith, and to make common witness to the world.

The Office of Theology and Worship of the Presbyterian Church (U.S.A.) noted the "Apostolic Faith" studies, consultations, and publications emerging from the World Council of Churches. Although the Office was not part of the Council's process, it embarked on a series of quadrennial theological convocations to explore the Nicene Creed in a North American context. In 1995 the first convocation, "We Believe in One Lord Jesus Christ," was held in Pittsburgh. The convocation explored central creedal affirmations concerning Jesus Christ as well as a number of contemporary problems and possibilities. In 1999 the second convocation was held in Charlotte and San Francisco. "We Believe in the Holy Spirit, the Lord, the Giver of Life," again featured addresses on creedal affirmations and on contemporary issues. The addresses from this convocation are collected as essays in this volume, together with sermons preached in the rich worship that is at the heart of all Theology and Worship convocations, conferences, and consultations. The final convocation in the series, "We Believe in One God," is scheduled for Pittsburgh in 2003.

The order of the convocations is not conventional, following neither the creedal Father–Son–Holy Spirit sequence nor the benedictory sequence of recent confessions: Son–Father–Holy Spirit. However, the Son–Holy Spirit–Father order of convocations may display more clearly the Trinitarian character of the Creed and each of its "articles." In particular, reserving the first article until last may help to make clear that the "one God" is not a generic deity, floating above the particularity of Jesus Christ and the immediacy of the Holy Spirit. At any rate, each of the convocations is explicitly and fully Trinitarian, an expression of the apostolic faith.

Fire and Wind's initial essay, "The Spirit and the Creed," provides both historical and contemporary context for the Creed and its confession in the church. The book then proceeds in three sections. The first section, "We Believe in . . . ," contains essays that explore four central affirmations of the Creed's third article. They are not historical examinations of a fourth-century creed, but rather contemporary explorations of the Creed's profession of faith in the Holy Spirit. Colin Gunton provides a substantial explication of the Trinity ("the Holy Spirit, . . . who with the Father and the Son is worshiped and glorified") that touches on historical, systematic, liturgical, and ethical issues. Cynthia Campbell focuses on Spirit and scripture ("the Holy Spirit, who has spoken through the prophets"), giving a striking, contemporary account of scripture and its interpretation. Ecclesiology is Miroslav Volf's concern ("one holy catholic and apostolic church"). He does not confine the issue within institutional frameworks, but widens its horizon to embrace the mission of the church within the reign of God. Leanne Van Dyk concludes the first section with an evocative, baptismal look at salvation from the perspective of the Spirit ("one baptism for the forgiveness of sins").

The second section takes up several pressing contemporary issues relating to renewed ecclesial and cultural interest in the Spirit. Gregory Love responds to the question, "Why the Holy Spirit Now?" by taking a critical look at both the promise and the peril of recent interest in the Spirit. Willie Jennings embarks on a bold exploration of the relationship between the Holy Spirit and the human spirit by route of the reality of self-deception ("Holy Spirit and Human Spirit: Overcoming a Deceived Heart"). Ellen Charry's passionate concern for children is at the heart of "The Trinity and the Christian Life," providing a renewed bond between doctrinal theology and spiritual formation. Finally, Elizabeth Nordquist tackles a contemporary concern head-on by inquiring into the relationship between "The Holy Spirit and Spiritual Formation."

The convocation on the Holy Spirit was marked throughout by worship. Scripture, psalms and hymns, preaching, and sacraments shaped a cycle of daily prayer. Rich worship cannot be captured on printed pages of liturgical orders, but publishing sermons that were preached by Craig Barnes, Linda Loving, Nancy Copeland-Payton, and Gregory Busby may give some sense of the convocation's character.

I am deeply grateful to my colleagues in the Office of Theology and Worship, whose energy, intelligence, imagination, and love serve the church faithfully. I am especially indebted to Associate for Theology Eunice McGarrahan—"Junior" to her many friends—who labored tirelessly, creatively, and graciously to make the Office of Theology and Worship convocations successful, both substantively and logistically.

I am also indebted to Tom Long and David Dobson of Geneva Press. Tom's vision for publishing books of service to the church was wide enough to include a collection of convocation addresses on the Holy Spirit. David's patience and skill were sufficient to translate vision into reality.

I can only begin to express my debt to my wife, Valerie, whose faith and faithfulness challenge my mind, fill my heart, and deepen my soul. "But this dedication is for others to read: These are private words addressed to you in public."

JOSEPH D. SMALL

Third Sunday of Easter, 2001

NOTES

1. T. S. Eliot, "A Dedication to My Wife," in *T. S. Eliot Collected Poems 1909–1962* (New York: Harcourt Brace Jovanovich, 1971), p. 221.

The Spirit and the Creed

Joseph D. Small

The first great ecumenical council of the church convened in A.D. 325 at Nicaea, a city near the imperial residence at Nicomedia. Over three hundred bishops gathered to resolve a controversy that threatened the peace, unity, and purity of the church. Church-dividing issues in our time are likely to be cultural and political, but the dispute tearing the fourth-century church apart was theological. The great theological controversy, involving ordinary Christians as well as priests and bishops, focused on the very being of God—specifically, the unity of the Son with the Father. The alternatives were stark. Is the Son fully divine—commensurate with the Father—as well as fully human? Or is the Son subordinate to the Father—a created being? Although the issue was theological, the debate was not abstract, for the issue went to the heart of Christians' understanding of God and of their own salvation.

The controversy centered on the views of Arius, a priest in Alexandria. Arius was a good thinker and a compelling preacher, who was eager to advocate God's oneness in the face of the surrounding culture's pervasive polytheism. He became convinced that the unity of God could be preserved only by excluding all distinctions from the divine nature. Thus, Arius preached and taught that the affirmation of God's oneness necessitated a lesser status for Jesus Christ and the Holy Spirit. While the Son and the Spirit were "divine," they remained created beings, subordinate to the one and only God. They were superior to all other created beings, of course, but they were not "God." "We know there is one God," said Arius and his associates, "the only unbegotten, only eternal, only without beginning, only true . . ."[1] For the Arians, this strong affirmation of the one true God necessitated a lesser status for the Son: "The Son, begotten timelessly by the Father and created before ages and established, was not before he was begotten. . . . He is neither eternal nor co-eternal nor co-unbegotten with the Father, nor does he have his being together with the Father."[2]

It was certainly not Arius's intention to denigrate Christ, for he venerated the Son as a divine mediator between God and humankind. Yet his desire to protect the oneness of God by preventing Father, Son, and Holy Spirit from being perceived as three gods led Arius to deny the unity of God the Father and God the Son. The response from Arius's bishop, Alexander, was swift and strong. In an encyclical letter, Alexander wrote: "What they assert in utter contrariety to the Scriptures, and wholly of their own devising, is as follows: . . . [A]ccording to their philosophy, 'the Son is a creature and a work; He is neither like the Father in essence, nor is the Father's true Word or His true Wisdom, but indeed one of His works and creatures.'"[3] The dispute between Arius and those who defended the unity of God the Father and God the Son was not a quiet intellectual disputation. Charges of heresy were hurled about publicly by both sides, and Christians throughout the Roman Empire were drawn into the struggle. Eventually, formal heresy charges against Arius were sustained by Alexander. The difference between the positions of Alexander and Arius was symbolized by the absence or presence of the little Greek letter "iota." Is the Son of the *same* substance (*homoousios*) as the Father, or of *similar* substance (*homoiousios*) to the Father?

The issue, now focused on the differing positions of Arius and Alexander, threatened to split the Christian church. The dispute went far deeper than scholarly or ecclesiastical quibbling over an insignificant distinction, for the question cut to the heart of Christian confidence in salvation and the character of Christian existence. Could Christians believe that Christ was "true God," and therefore trust that the salvation announced and accomplished in Jesus Christ was God's gracious will? Or was Jesus Christ something less than God, so that God's will remained mysterious—an uncertain purpose behind, above, and beyond the words and deeds of Jesus Christ? Were men and women who were "in Christ" thereby reconciled to God? Or was there another step that had to be taken in order to be reconciled to the still-hidden God who dwelt behind Christ? Had God come to humankind in the person of Jesus Christ? Or had God remained aloof, only sending an emissary?

Twenty-first-century theological differences are not drawn along "orthodox/Arian" lines, yet the stakes are similar. The unity of God—Father, Son, and Holy Spirit—is the essential guarantee that we are able to know God truly. If Jesus Christ is not "truly God" as well as "truly human," then he is merely a path toward a God who remains essentially unknown. Similarly, if "the Spirit" is not the Holy Spirit of God, then our deepest spiritual experience is not an encounter with the one true God, but only an approach to the God who remains essentially distant. Now, as then, the church's understanding and experience of God depends on its understanding of Jesus Christ and of the Holy Spirit, and on its affirmation of the one true God—Father, Son, and Holy Spirit.

The broad historical outline of the first great ecumenical council of the church is well-known. Constantine, the first Christian emperor, convened a council of the church's bishops to resolve the dispute and restore peace to the church. There is no doubt that Constantine's motives were political as well as theological and ecclesial; he was concerned for the unity of the empire as well as the unity of the church and its faith. Yet Constantine's mixed motives do not detract from the gravity of the issue or from the significance of the council's decisions.

The story of the Council of Nicaea has come to be seen as the narrative of orthodoxy's triumph: the partisans of the "heresiarch" Arius were defeated by the good Bishop Alexander, and the church's faith was clearly articulated in the council's Creed. It is not quite that simple, of course. What we now know as the "Nicene Creed" did not even take final form until the Council of Constantinople in A.D. 381—which is why the creed is more properly called "The Nicene-Constantinopolitan Creed."[4] The fundamental issue was not even settled decisively in 325, for the dispute continued to rage in the years between Nicaea and Constantinople. Throughout this contentious period, emperors, popes, patriarchs, bishops, priests, and ordinary Christians were drawn into a continuous struggle. In the fifty-six years between Nicaea and

Constantinople, no fewer than twelve regional councils tended to support the views . . . of Arius! Athanasius, the great hero of the orthodox position, was banished and restored five separate times as the battle tended first one way and then the other. Yet the decades led toward the decisive orthodox professions of the Council of Constantinople. The bishops meeting at Constantinople introduced refinements of the 325 creed's second article concerning the Son, and made a small addition to the creed's first article concerning the Father. But the most dramatic change occurred in the third article.

The Nicene Creed of 325 followed its precise affirmations of "the one Lord, Jesus Christ" with a terse, "and [we believe] in the Holy Spirit." Nothing more came after this minimal "third article" except a list of anathemas against those who held to the erroneous views of the Arians. The Council of Nicaea was concerned with establishing the unity of God the Father and God the Son, and so did not give explicit attention to the church's faith in the Holy Spirit. Once the full parity of Father and Son was established, however, similar matters had to be articulated about the Holy Spirit. Was the Holy Spirit fully God, or was the Spirit a lesser, created being?

The Council of Constantinople did not address the issue of the Holy Spirit by using the technical philosophical categories of the second article—*ousias* and *homoousios*. Instead, the bishops employed biblical, narrative language to express the divine being of the Holy Spirit. Thus, the sparse words of Nicaea, "And [we believe] in the Holy Spirit," were fleshed out in rich, highly suggestive words and phrases:

> We believe in the Holy Spirit, the Lord, the giver of life,
>   who proceeds from the Father
>   who with the Father and the Son is worshiped and glorified,
>   who has spoken through the prophets.
> We believe in one holy catholic and apostolic Church.
> We acknowledge one baptism for the forgiveness of sins.
> We look for the resurrection of the dead,
>   and the life of the world to come. Amen.

THE RULE OF FAITH

The "well-known" story of the Nicene Creed may lead to a false impression of church life and of the genesis of the Creed itself. The story may suggest that the business of the early church was the development of doctrine, with bishops and archbishops debating among themselves to sort out true faith and heresy, establishing universal criteria of truth for the ages. Alternatively, the story may encourage the impression that ecclesiastical and imperial politics came together to suppress diversity by establishing a "Constantinian" uniformity in church and empire. Both impressions may grow from the notion that the Creed was "composed" in 325, emerging full-blown from the deliberations of the church's bishops. The Nicene Creed was not an innovation, however, for its roots were deep in the church's baptismal life.

Throughout the years of controversy leading up to the Council of Nicaea, people on both sides defended their doctrinal positions by referring to the faith they had received from their bishops, often quoting creedlike summaries of Christian faith. Arius himself appealed to the teaching of certain prominent bishops, identifying his position with theirs by stating that they also taught "that God exists without beginning before the Son."[5] The numerous references to the bishops' teaching all alluded to the church's method of training persons for baptism and initiation into the church.

In the church's early centuries, new converts were admitted to the community as "hearers of the word"—*catechumens*—for a three-year period of instruction in the faith prior to baptism. During this period, catechumens could attend the first part of Lord's day worship— prayers, hymns, psalms, scripture, and preaching—but not the Eucharist. The extended period of initiation, climaxed by the bishop's instruction during Lent, involved the scriptures, the community's life of prayer and praise, the calling to a new way of living, and the church's rule of faith. Shortly before Easter, the catechumens were examined. Hippolytus's *Apostolic Tradition* describes the ancient practice:

> And when they are chosen who are set apart to receive baptism let their life be examined, whether they lived piously while catechumens, whether they "honored the widows," whether they visited the sick, whether they have fulfilled every good work. If those who bring them bear witness to them that they have done thus, let them hear the gospel.[6]

On the Thursday before Easter, the candidates bathed, then fasted on Friday and Saturday. Beginning at sundown on Saturday, the whole night was spent in vigil, with readings, prayers, and instruction. On Easter, as the first light of dawn appeared in the East, the candidates descended into a large baptismal pool of running water where they renounced Satan and all his works. They then confessed the faith and were baptized. Their confession of faith was structured by its baptismal setting, for the shape of baptismal faith emerged from the commission of the risen Lord: "Go therefore and make disciples of all nations, baptizing them in the name of the Father and of the Son and of the Holy Spirit, and teaching them to obey everything that I have commanded you" (Matt. 28:19–20).

The church understood that baptism was not its own action, but the church's faithful response to its Lord's commission. This commission did more than institute baptism, however. It also gave baptism its meaning. Baptizing "in the name of the Father and of the Son and of the Holy Spirit" gave baptism a Trinitarian structure that set forth the Trinitarian being of God and so proclaimed the fullness of the church's Trinitarian faith. The name of the triune God was not a mere formula, but an expression of the substance of Christian faith. The nature and action of the one God—Father, Son, and Holy Spirit—became, in baptism, the focus of Christian identity for the church and for each baptized person:

> And [when] he [who is to be baptised] goes down to the water, let him who baptises lay [his] hand on him saying thus:
> > Dost thou believe in God the Father Almighty?
> And he who is being baptised shall say: I believe.
> Let him forthwith baptise him once, having his hand laid upon his head.
> And after this let him say:
> > Dost thou believe in Christ Jesus, the Son of God,
> > Who was born of the Holy Spirit and the Virgin Mary,
> > Who was crucified in the days of Pontius Pilate,
> > and died,
> > And rose on the third day living from the dead
> > And ascended into the heavens,
> > And sat down at the right hand of the Father,
> > And will come to judge the living and the dead?
> And when he says: I believe, let him baptise him the second time.
> And again let him say:
> > Dost thou believe in the Holy Spirit in the Holy Church,
> > And the resurrection of the flesh?
> And he who is being baptised shall say: I believe. And so let him baptise him the third time.[7]

The genesis of the Nicene Creed does not lie in the need for standards of doctrinal orthodoxy, then, but in the summaries of Christian faith taught to new believers by their local bishops and confessed at baptism. These standard summaries were specific to each bishop's diocese, and so their details varied from place to place. Yet the summaries were not widely divergent, for all were instances of the "Rule of Faith"—*regula fidei*—that provided the church with a norm of Christian faith and practice. As early as the second century, Irenaeus set forth an already traditional summary of Christian faith, concluding with the assertion that "Having received this preaching and this faith, as I have said, the Church, although scattered in the whole world, carefully preserves it, as if living in one house. She believes these things [everywhere] alike, as if she had but one heart and one soul, and preaches them harmoniously, teaches them, and hands them down, as if she had but one mouth."[8] We may recognize in Irenaeus's images an idealized portrait of the church's unanimity, but this should not diminish our awareness of the church's substantial agreement about the shape of its faith. The *regula fidei,* its expression in catechesis, and its summaries in baptismal confessions of faith, provided a basic digest of the Christian story and the focal point of Christian identity. The rule of faith shaped the instruction of new Christians and provided the substance of their baptismal confession.

While expressions of the rule of faith, the catechetical teaching of the bishops, and the baptismal confessions were not "fixed," they summarized the same scriptural story and shared the familiar three-part structure, with clauses about God the Father, the Son of God, and the Holy Spirit. Thus, while the church's faith was self-consciously biblical and consistently Trinitarian, the *regula fidei* did not articulate an explicit doctrine of the Trinity. Instead, its narrative structure in both teaching and liturgy told a story, and that story summarized the gospel through a synopsis of the scriptures.

Over a century before the Council of Nicaea, Tertullian provided a striking rendition of the *regula fidei*:

> The Rule of Faith—to state here and now what we maintain—is of course that by which we believe that there is but one God, who is none other than the Creator of the world, who produced everything from nothing through

his Word, sent forth before all things; that this Word is called his Son, and in the name of God was seen in divers ways by the patriarchs, was ever heard in the prophets and finally was brought down by the Spirit and Power of God the Father into the Virgin Mary, was made flesh in her womb, was born of her and lived as Jesus Christ; who thereafter proclaimed a new law and a new promise of the kingdom of heaven, worked miracles, was crucified, on the third day rose again, was caught up into heaven and sat down at the right hand of the Father; that he sent in his place the power of the Holy Spirit to guide believers; that he will come with glory to take the saints up into the fruition of the life eternal and the heavenly promises and to judge the wicked to everlasting fire, after the resurrection of both good and evil with the restoration of their flesh.[9]

Tertullian followed his rendition of the *regula fidei* with the counsel that "Provided the essence of the rule is not disturbed, you may seek and discuss as much as you like. You may give full reign to your itching curiosity where any point seems unsettled and ambiguous or dark and obscure."[10]

The citations from Tertullian demonstrate both clear antecedent to the Nicene Creed and the need for the Creed. Indeed, while the *regula fidei*'s summary of the faith provided the building blocks of the Creed, it surely left some things unsettled and ambiguous, even dark and obscure. Chief among the ambiguities that needed clarification were the relationships of the three main "characters" in the story: Father, Son, and Holy Spirit.

WE BELIEVE IN THE HOLY SPIRIT

The explicit issue in the Arian controversy was the relationship between the Son and the Father. Although the full divinity of the Son was established in principle at Nicaea, there was no parallel affirmation of the full divinity of the Holy Spirit. The church had always assumed the continuing presence of the Holy Spirit in its life, inspiring and sanctifying its members, priests, and bishops. There was little doubt among believers that in the presence of the Spirit, God was at work in the church. But it was inevitable that the Arian controversy, while centered on the Son, would provoke a parallel debate about the divinity of the Spirit. The Arian heresy "speaks against the Word of God," wrote Athanasius, "and as a logical consequence profanes His Holy Spirit."[11] If the Son was a subordinate, created being as the Arians asserted, surely the Spirit was a subordinate, created being as well. In the decades following Nicaea, the Arians attacked the Spirit's divinity, earning for themselves the epithet *pneumatomachoi*—"fighters against the Spirit." Athanasius and the "orthodox" Christians affirmed that the Holy Spirit is the Spirit of Christ within us, and so, as Christ is truly God, the Spirit must be truly God as well.

Basil the Great voiced the seriousness of the matter before the church. "All the weapons of war have been prepared against us; every intellectual missile is aimed at us. . . . But we will never surrender the truth; we will not betray the defense like cowards. The Lord has delivered to us a necessary and saving dogma: the Holy Spirit is to be ranked with the Father. Our opponents do not agree; instead they divide and tear away the Spirit from the Father, transforming His nature to that of a ministering spirit."[12]

The "orthodox" struggled to rank the Holy Spirit with the Father and the Son, yet neither Athanasius, nor the Cappadocians, nor the Nicene-Constantinopolitan Creed of 381 applied the term *homoousios* to the Holy Spirit. Instead, the traditional narrative language of the *regula fidei* was employed to give an account of the Spirit's movement in the church and the lives of the faithful. "I reckon that this 'glorifying' [of the Holy Spirit] is nothing else but the recounting of His own wonders," said Basil. "To describe His wonders gives Him the fullest glorification possible. The same is true for the God and Father of our Lord Jesus Christ and the Only-Begotten Son Himself; we are only able to glorify them by recounting their wonders to the best of our ability."[13]

THE NARRATIVE OF THE HOLY SPIRIT

The third article of the Nicene Creed—and of the Western Church's Apostles' Creed—may give the impression of being a few general affirmations about the Holy Spirit followed by a laundry list of disconnected doctrinal leftovers. The impression is a false one, however, for like the first two articles, the third provides a coherent narrative of God's being and action—a "recounting of God's wonders."

The Creed articulates belief in the one God who created all that is—heaven and earth, invisible reality as well as that which is accessible to the senses. This creating God is not the "clockmaker" of deism, who set the world in motion and then left it to function on its own. Rather, the Creator is "the Almighty" who continues to enact providential care over all that is. Neither is this creating God a monad, self-contained and self-sufficient. Rather, the Creator is "the Father," an intrinsically relational being who is Father and Son and Spirit, whose providential relationship to creation is exercised through the redemptive action of the Son and the Spirit.

The Creed articulates belief in the one Lord Jesus Christ, the Son who is of one being with the Father and through whom all was created. This Lord is not a distant cosmic ruler, but one who, through the power of the Holy Spirit, became part of our time and space for the sake of our salvation. The life, death, and resurrection of Jesus Christ is narrated in familiar human terms, climaxing with the proclamation of his heavenly rule and his promised coming to establish justice within an eternal reign.

If the narrative of God with us had stopped at the end of the Creed's second article, it might appear to be an account of "the good old days with God," times when God was present and active in human life. Did God become one with us for a brief, shining moment, only to withdraw into mystery until an indeterminate future? "No," says the Creed. God remains present and active among us as the Holy Spirit in our midst. This Holy Spirit is not God's vague spiritual presence, for the Spirit is none other than the "Lord, the giver of life," through whom the "one Lord, Jesus Christ" was incarnate. Thus, the Holy Spirit is worshiped and glorified *with* the Father and the Son, not apart from the whole economy of God.

Shortly before his death, Jesus assured his disciples, "I will not leave you orphaned" (John 14:18). He promised the continuing presence of "another Advocate, to be with you forever. This is the Spirit of truth. . . . You know him, because he abides with you, and he will be in you" (John 14:16,17). The Creed articulates God's continuous presence with humankind as the Holy Spirit abides with, among, and in the human community. The Spirit reveals the truth about God's

Way in the world, creating new human community, empowering the people of God, nurturing the church in faithfulness, and leading us in lives of love, joy, and peace.

The Nicene Creed's narrative of the Holy Spirit recounts the continuing action of the life-giving Spirit, who spoke and speaks through the scriptures, who forms the Christian community and shapes its character, who unites us to Christ's death and resurrection in baptism, who seals forgiveness and new life within us, and who fills us with hope for ourselves and for all creation. John Calvin, writing twelve centuries after Nicaea, sums it up well: "Thus through [the Holy Spirit] we come into communion with God, so that we in a way feel his life-giving power toward us. Our justification is his work; from him is power, sanctification, truth, grace, and every good thing that can be conceived."[14]

THE CREED AND THE SPIRIT

In a culture (and a church) that pays scant attention to the past, it is not immediately apparent why anyone should pay attention to the Nicene Creed. Even a condensed recitation of Nicaea's story may seem far more than is necessary to review the ancient past. What is the twenty-first-century relevance of a fourth-century creed? Most Christians now encounter the Creed, appropriately, in worship, yet many encounter it there as burden rather than gift. Kathleen Norris expresses the sentiment of many North American Christians when she says, "Of all the elements in a Christian worship service, the Creed, by compressing the wide range of faith and belief into a few words, can feel like a verbal strait jacket."[15]

In the great theological controversy of the fourth century, the Nicene Creed served to separate truth from error, orthodoxy from heresy. Although some in our time would like to use the Creed as a doctrinal test to identify those who are in error, its enduring significance does not lie in its function as a dividing line. The Creed continues to serve the church catholic by voicing the church's fundamental identity. By confessing the truth about God—Father, Son, and Holy Spirit—we say who we are as the people of God, the body of Christ, the community of the Holy Spirit. It is true enough that the Creed once inoculated believers against heresy and apostasy—and may do so still—but the more basic issue of the Creed was and is Christian identity. Who is God? Who are we? Does God care about us? How does God act in our lives? How, in God's grace, shall we live together? The Creed, like the Rule of Faith in which it is grounded, tells the story of God and ourselves, the story of redemption and new life.

To be sure, giving voice to Christian identity entails saying "No" to some things as well as "Yes" to others. Genuine confession of faith is always both affirmation of truth and denial of untruth. "If the Yes does not in some way contain the No," said Karl Barth, "it will not be the Yes of a confession. . . . If we have not the confidence to say *damnamus* [we refuse], then we might as well omit the *credimus* [we believe]."[16] The identity of a community as *Christian* entails renunciation of what is not from God as well as affirmation of God and God's new Way. Sometimes the "No" is explicit, as with the Theological Declaration of Barmen, sometimes it is implicit, as with the Nicene Creed. But always, in the community's struggle to define itself in fidelity to the grace of the Lord Jesus Christ, the love of God, and the communion of the Holy Spirit, it must say "Yes" to God's Way in the world, and "No" to the ways of the world apart from God.

The task of defining the appropriate center of Christian faith and faithfulness, and their appropriate boundaries, is not unique to some generations while absent from others. Rather, it is an ever-present and continuous process that draws from the past experience of the church as it presses toward hope in the future that God is bringing to be. Christopher Morse puts it well: "Memory and hope, story and promise, occur inseparably in the apostolic tradition. To keep the memory from blocking the hope (the temptation of conservatives), and to keep the hope from severing itself from the memory (the temptation of liberals) is the task of all dogmatics that seeks to be attentive to apostolic tradition."[17]

When we are attentive to the apostolic tradition as it is expressed in the Nicene Creed, we are struck by an interplay of universality and particularity. The Creed presents itself as an expression of the necessary catholicity of the church's belief, described by the ancient motto *quod ubique, quod semper, quod ab omnibus, creditum est* (what is held everywhere, always, and by all is to be believed). Clearly, this formula is not meant as an objective statement of empirical fact, but it does express the truth that some elements of Christian faith and faithfulness are essential to Christian identity—that without which no community would be identifiably Christian. Yet within the Creed's universality we find particularities of fourth-century Greco-Roman culture. The Greek philosophical categories of *ousia* and *homoousios* (or their Latin "equivalents," *substantia* and *persona*) may even be difficult to express in contemporary language. The Creed is both universal and particular. We respond to its universality by saying the Creed as it has been given to us, joining our voices to the witness of the church throughout time and space. And yet, as we receive its witness faithfully, we respond to its particularity by interpreting the Creed in this time and place.

Interpretation of the Creed has become an urgent task in our time and place. In a diverse, highly segmented society such as ours, patterns of belief are no longer shaped by customary articulations or associations. Convictions and actions have become matters of individual choice and private decision. There are no paths that people must follow or authorities to which they are accountable—whether families, or advisers, or systems, or institutions. Instead, individuals assume that *they* are the authority deciding which of multiple possibilities to choose. What is true of our culture is also true within the church. The contemporary church is not a community of shared certainty in commonly acknowledged truths. The church has never been a uniform community of unanimous views, of course. Even a casual reading of the New Testament letters is sufficient to confirm that the church has been characterized by diversity from the beginning. Yet the New Testament letters assume that, within the matrix of rich human diversities, unity in the faith is a central intention of Christian community. That assumption does not go unquestioned among us.

We live in a pluralistic world, and so we desire a church that is inclusive of the world's rich diversity. Our celebration of diversity goes beyond appreciation for the natural variety of race, ethnicity, gender, and personal gifts, however. We also make room in the church for a wide variety of preferences, opinions, convictions, and beliefs. Many people within the church simply assume that theological and moral truths are different for different Christians. Since a wide variety of beliefs emerges from a wide range of personal and communal experience, even *Christian* beliefs are thought to be diverse.

In a pluralistic church, interpretation of the Creed is an essential task. The intention of interpretation is certainly not to impose dogmatic formulations or compel assent to an institutional orthodoxy. Instead, common attention to the Creed can engage Christians in a shared search for the truth about God and ourselves—truth that can liberate us from idolatry and self-deception, truth that can set us free to love God and our neighbors. The Nicene Creed is especially suitable for shared inquiry, precisely because it has been the most nearly "universal" expression of Christian faith for almost seventeen centuries. Orthodox churches of the East, the Catholic Church and Protestant churches of the West, as well as younger churches of the South, have joined their voices to confess together the apostolic faith. This primacy of time and space gives to the Nicene Creed a claim on our attention. Through the Creed, we are called by our forebears in the faith to join them in a common search for shared faith and faithfulness.

THE SPIRIT AND THE CREED

The urgency of interpretation may be most apparent in the Creed's third article. There is no doubt that our time and place is experiencing a remarkable fascination with the Spirit.[18] The worldwide Pentecostal movement, barely a century old, is considered by many to be the fourth great Christian ecclesial family, after the Orthodox, Catholic, and Protestant. Since the 1960s, most mainline Protestant churches have experienced charismatic renewal movements, with intense experiences of the Spirit and renewed appropriation of spiritual gifts. More recently, "spiritual formation" has become a staple of mainline church life, complete with spiritual directors, *lectio divina,* and labyrinths. Spirituality is not confined to Christian churches, however, for our culture is now home to a plethora of Eastern and New Age spiritualities. Buddhist meditation techniques, crystals and pyramids, Celtic traditions, and "channeling" all appear on the spiritual smorgasbord, ready to be sampled by people who experience an unsatisfied need at the core of their being.

There is no doubt that our objectified, differentiated, segmented, privatized, market-driven society creates a hollowness that yearns to be filled. It is precisely this human yearning that may become narcissism, however. Aspiration may produce a real and present danger of reducing "spirituality" to "religiosity," complete with the familiar hazards of self-projection and idolatry. The Christian version of this danger may be detected in a growing tendency to use "Spirit" as a generalized reference to the divine, thus avoiding the particularity of Jesus Christ and eliding distinctively Trinitarian language.

Attention to the Creed's affirmations of the Holy Spirit may help us to receive the rich specificity of Christian faith that goes beyond vague references to "Spirit," locating the fulfillment of human need in the gracious action of the triune God. The Spirit of the Creed is "Holy Spirit," which is to say, the Spirit of "God, the Father, the Almighty." The Spirit of the Creed is "the Lord, the giver of life," which is to say the "Spirit of Christ." This identification of the Holy Spirit as the Spirit of God and the Spirit of Christ is not the product of an abstract theological calculus, but a reflection of the whole range of biblical testimony. The narrative of God's Way is the narrative of the Holy Spirit, from the waters of Creation to the heavenly invitation of Revelation. Thus, the Holy Spirit is worshiped and glorified *with* the Father and the Son, not apart from the Trinitarian fullness of God.

Just as the Holy Spirit is not separable from the Father and the Son, so the Holy Spirit is not set apart from the testimony of the scriptures. The Holy Spirit "has spoken through the prophets" and continues to speak through the scriptures, which in turn bear witness to the Holy Spirit's work in Israel, in Jesus of Nazareth, and in the church. Thus, the Spirit is not who we wish a spirit to be, but rather the Holy Spirit who is the revealed One as well as the revealer.

Just as the Holy Spirit is not separable from the Father and the Son nor set apart from the scriptures, so the Holy Spirit is not detached from the church. The one holy catholic and apostolic church is not the product of human striving, an accomplishment of human faithfulness. It is the Holy Spirit who creates and sustains and reforms a communion that lives in the grace of the Lord Jesus Christ and the love of God. The Holy Spirit is not confined to the church, of course, but the church is the "provisional demonstration of what God intends for all of humanity."[19] Thus, the Spirit's activity beyond the church is neither an alternative to the church nor a disjunctive mode of being.

Just as the Holy Spirit is not separable from the Father and the Son, nor set apart from the scriptures, nor detached from the church, so the Holy Spirit is not aloof from our deepest experience. Our forgiveness, acceptance, reconciliation, redemption—our salvation—is sealed in our lives through the Spirit, who unites us to Christ in the waters of baptism. The Holy Spirit is God with and for us in one baptism for the forgiveness of sins. The Holy Spirit remains God with us and for us as we live our baptisms by forgiving as we have been forgiven. In this way, the Holy Spirit is not the locus of my private spirituality, but the giver of life together with others, enemies as well as friends.

Finally, the Holy Spirit is not remote from our fears and hopes, both for ourselves and for the whole creation. Nor is the Spirit irrelevant to the fears and hopes of people beyond the communion of the church. The resurrection of the dead and the life of the world to come are the sure and certain work of the Holy Spirit. We do not have to rely on technique or technology, on capability or power, for God's Holy Spirit nourishes hope "that the creation itself will be set free from its bondage to decay" (Rom. 8:21). *Veni Creator Spiritus.*

These brief concluding comments do not pretend to be adequate interpretations of the Creed's affirmations of the Holy Spirit. They are merely the briefest invitation to the church to engage in the interpretation of the communion of the Holy Spirit that can bind us in faith, hope, and love. The following essays in this book are richer explorations of creedal affirmations, cultural and ecclesial contexts, and faithful proclamation. In addition to these contributions, I wish to draw attention to a recent "interpretation of the Nicene Creed." Although not formally—or even intentionally—an interpretation, the Presbyterian Church (U.S.A.)'s "A Brief Statement of Faith" (1991) gives narrative voice to the church's beliefs about the Holy Spirit. Criticized by some because "it contained nothing new" (as if confessions of faith are supposed to be novel!), the Brief Statement's third article is a faithful expression of the church's apostolic faith. Note how the Nicene Creed's affirmations are picked up, reordered, elaborated, applied, and even enriched:

We trust in God the Holy Spirit,
    everywhere the giver and renewer of life.
The Spirit justifies us by grace through faith,

sets us free to accept ourselves and to love God and neighbor,
and binds us together with all believers
in one body of Christ, the Church.
The same Spirit
who inspired the prophets and apostles
rules our faith and life in Christ through Scripture,
engages us through the Word proclaimed,
claims us in the waters of baptism,
feeds us with the bread of life and the cup of salvation,
and calls women and men to all ministries of the Church.
In a broken and fearful world
the Spirit gives us courage
to pray without ceasing,
to witness among all peoples to Christ as Lord and Savior,
to unmask idolatries in Church and culture,
to hear the voices of peoples long silenced,
and to work with others for justice, freedom, and peace.
In gratitude to God, empowered by the Spirit,
we strive to serve Christ in our daily tasks
and to live holy and joyful lives,
even as we watch for God's new heaven and new earth,
praying, "Come, Lord Jesus!" . . .

Glory be to the Father, and to the Son, and to the Holy Spirit. Amen.[20]

NOTES

1. "The Confession of the Arians Addressed to Alexander of Alexandria," in *Christology of the Later Fathers,* ed. Edward R. Handy (Philadelphia: Westminster Press, 1954), p. 332.
2. Ibid., p. 333.
3. "Encyclical Letter of Alexander of Alexandria and His Clergy," in *A New Eusebius,* ed. J. Stevenson (London: S.P.C.K., 1965), p. 343.
4. To complicate matters further, the records of the Council of Constantinople do not contain the creed itself. The text of "The Niceno-Constantinopolitan Creed" does not appear until the Council of Chalcedon, A.D. 451!
5. "The Letter of Arius to Eusebius of Nicomedia," *Christology of the Later Fathers,* p. 330.
6. Hippolytus, *The Apostolic Tradition,* ed. Gregory Dix and Henry Chadwick (London: Alban Press, 1937/1991), xx.1–2, pp. 30f.
7. Ibid., xxi.12–18, pp. 36f.
8. Irenaeus, *Adversus Haereses,* 1.10.2., in *Early Christian Fathers,* ed. Cyril C. Richardson (Philadelphia: Westminster Press, 1953), p. 360.

9. Tertullian, "Prescriptions against Heretics," 13, in *Early Latin Theology*, ed. S. L. Greenslade (Philadelphia: Westminster Press, 1956), pp. 39f.

10. Ibid., 14, p. 40.

11. Athanasius, "Letter to Maximus" (c. 371), in *Nicene and Post-Nicene Fathers*, vol. 4, ed. Philip Schaff and Henry Wace (Peabody, Mass.: Hendrickson, 1892/1994), p. 567.

12. St. Basil the Great, *On the Holy Spirit,* trans. David Anderson (Crestwood, N. Y.: St. Vladimir's Seminary, 1997), 10.25, pp. 45f.

13. Ibid., 23.54, p. 86.

14. John Calvin, *Institutes of the Christian Religion*, ed. John T. McNeill, trans. Ford Lewis Battles (Philadelphia: Westminster Press, 1960), 1.13.14., p. 139.

15. Kathleen Norris, *Amazing Grace* (New York: Riverhead Books, 1998), p. 205.

16. Karl Barth, *Church Dogmatics* I/2 (Edinburgh: T. & T. Clark, 1956), pp. 631, 630.

17. Christopher Morse, *Not Every Spirit* (New York: Trinity Press International, 1992), p. 48.

18. Thus, the recent book by Harvey Cox, barometer of cultural-religious trends, *Fire from Heaven: The Rise of Pentecostal Spirituality and the Reshaping of Religion in the Twenty-first Century* (Reading, Mass.: Addison-Wesley Publishing Co., 1995).

19. Presbyterian Church (U.S.A.), *Book of Order* (Louisville, Ky.: Office of the General Assembly, 2000), G-3.0200.

20. Presbyterian Church (U.S.A.) "A Brief Statement of Faith." *Book of Confessions: Study Edition* (Louisville, Ky.: Geneva Press, 1999), 10.4, 10.6, p. 342.

WE BELIEVE IN . . .

We Believe in the Holy Spirit, Who with the Father and the Son Is Worshiped and Glorified

Colin Gunton

DIVINE BEING AND ACTION

The God of biblical faith is a God of particular action. Israel, Jesus, and the church are at once typical of the way God works in the world, and more than merely typical, for they determine our understanding of how his acts take place. It is also the case that the creeds were formed in a particular historical development, though in this case the development is more ambiguous. It is possible to read the development of the creeds in a suspicious way, especially when you remember some of the political contexts, with the Council of Nicaea assembled for the peace of the Roman Empire as well as—some would say more than—for the well-being of the church. But for the most part it is perhaps, as Barth liked to remark, *hominum confusione, dei providentia*: by human confusion and divine providence. The creeds emerged out of a particular story of worship and life, of thought and dispute. They developed out of the struggles of the church to be itself and to communicate its gospel in the world of which it was a part. Only by beginning there can we begin to learn how we should be the church in the strangely similar world of which we are a part. (Of course, everybody says how different and unique the modern world is, and that is true also. I shall return to that point at the end.)

The emergence of the affirmation, ". . . the Holy Spirit, . . . who with the Father and the Son is worshiped and glorified" was by no means a straightforward matter. From one point of view, there seems to be very little difficulty, if we listen to scripture, in concluding that the Spirit of God is divine. All the things the Spirit does are things done by God: he breathes over the waters of creation, inspires the prophets and the church, raises Jesus from the dead, and is poured out on the church at Pentecost, in anticipation of the very end of all things. It is worth noting that according to one difficult saying of Jesus, sin against the Spirit—the Spirit of truth—is the only unforgivable sin (Matt. 12: 31).

We might say—and I want to stress this point—that very often for scripture the Spirit is God being eschatological. For the New Testament especially, wherever the Spirit is, there the conditions of the last times are anticipated: in the church being led into all truth, in the anticipation of the communion of the last days, in all kinds of ways in which the end is promised and anticipated—above all, of course, in the resurrection of Jesus. The Spirit is the one, as the Eastern Orthodox tradition likes to stress, who raised Jesus from the dead, in fulfillment of the promise inherent in Ezekiel 37: 1–14. This can also be illustrated from Romans 8 and from Paul's description of the Spirit as the "down payment"—a monetary image speaking of the first installment and guarantee of final redemption (2 Cor. 1:22; 5:5; Eph. 1:14).

But perhaps the most interesting and extended illustration is to be taken from the book of Revelation. "I, John, . . . was on the island called Patmos on account of the word of God and the testimony of Jesus. I was in the Spirit on the Lord's day . . . (Rev. 1:9–10, RSV). Being in the Spirit means, perhaps most obviously but also dangerously being in an inspired state—dangerously because we are always in danger of mistaking the Spirit of God for a force or an experience of some kind.[1] But I think that John means much more than that. It is the reference to the Lord's day that is significant, for it refers to worship, and it is through sharing mysteriously in the worship of his separated fellow Christians that John is enabled also to share the worship of heaven and the vision both of what is happening now and what is going to happen at the end. The Holy Spirit reveals to the seer at once the present and the future as it shapes the present, but only as a function of the communion of the church in which he is enabled to share.

In that light, it seems far easier to see the Spirit as divine than it is to see the man, Jesus of Nazareth, as such. A man is, for scripture in general, fairly obviously not divine, and that is why to confess Jesus, the crucified teacher and prophet, as Lord and God (John 20:28) is on the face of it far more difficult than to understand the Holy Spirit to be divine. Indeed, it has been suggested that perhaps the one attempted definition of God in the New Testament is that "God is Spirit" (though whether "God is love" is also a kind of definition and how it coheres with this is an interesting question).[2] And yet what might appear to be obvious was not, for the most part, historically the case. It was "for the most part" because the second-century theologian, Irenaeus, to whom we shall return, described both the Son and the Spirit as the "two hands of God," God himself in action, and clearly believed in the eternal divinity of the Spirit.[3] But Irenaeus was untroubled by considerations that troubled others (that is his unique genius), and after him it came to seem to some far from obvious that the Spirit was equal in rank with the Father and Son. It was not until after the full divinity of the Son of God had been established with much agony and argument that a similar process of discernment was applied to the Spirit.

Here, we have to distinguish two aspects of the problem. The first concerns the being of God. Is the Spirit a distinct person within God's being? The difficulty here lies in the fact that the world in which all this was hammered out tended to think in hierarchies, in layers, so that it was almost impossible for them—and it is here that we have to exercise a great deal of historical imagination—not to suppose that God the Father is fully divine, the Son rather less so, and the Spirit even lower. The shape of the problem as it developed can be seen in the work of Origen of Alexandria in the third century. For Origen, God the Son was a second God, derivatively divine, we might say, and the Spirit was the highest of the creatures, sent by God to sanctify the believer.[4] We must beware of dismissing this too easily. The point about these theological problems is that because they concern the being of God, there is no simple solution. The complexity is apparent if we again refer to the scriptural characterization of God.

It is almost a commonplace of New Testament scholarship that when the New Testament speaks of God, *simpliciter,* it usually can be taken to be referring to God the Father. Similarly, there are respects in which Jesus and the Spirit are subordinate to the Father. In John's Gospel, for example, Jesus subordinates himself to the Father: he is sent to do the Father's work, to obey his will in Gethsemane, and later to ask the Father to send "another comforter," the Spirit. Similarly in 1 Corinthians 15, the point of Jesus' ministry and reign at the Father's right hand is, at the end, to hand all things over to God the Father, so that God may be all in all. What is technically called "subordination-ism," the teaching that the Son and the Spirit are in some way less divine than God the Father, *seems* to have some support in scripture, so that from one point of view it is not obvious that some form of sub-ordinationism is wrong. It seems a very satisfactory way to guarantee God's unity, something essential to the faith, for there is but one God and one gospel.

There is, however, a second side to the question (as always in the-ology!), and a brief outline of that will take us to the very heart of the matter. Christianity is what it is because it is a gospel, and that gospel implies, requires, that God act in and toward his world. The problem is this: If we attribute particular actions in the world to the Son and the Holy Spirit—as when the book of Acts says things like "It has seemed good to the Holy Spirit and to us"—is that effectively to divide up the action of God? Can we really say that the Father does some things, the Son others, and the Spirit yet others?[5] This problem comes to a head in some of the creeds, for example, the so-called Apos-tles' Creed: "I believe in God the Father Almighty, Maker of heaven and earth, . . . and in . . . his only Son . . . who was born . . ." This raises the question of what is called "modalism": that Father, Son, and Spirit are different modes of the one being of God. And the problem with that is that it suggests that the real God is an unknown some-thing lying behind the three agents but not really like any of them.

As in all theology, we are on a knife edge, or, we might say, a nar-row path with precipices on each side. On one side, we deny the unity of God, and make it appear that there are three gods; on the other, we cause the distinctions of the three to disappear into some underlying undifferentiated deity.[6] On the whole, our Western tradition has tended to the latter, so to stress the unity of God's action that it becomes difficult to do justice to its diversity. This is partly responsible for some prominent features of church life over the centuries. First, we have not known what to make of the Spirit's action, and tended to depersonalize it, speaking rather of "grace" as a sort of fluid poured into the person (the Catholic tendency); or we have identified the Spirit's action with warm feelings, subjective inspirations, and the like—a sort of religious fix (the Protestant side). Second, we have notoriously neglected the work of the Spirit in our life and thinking, and that is why there have been outbreaks of Pentecostal church life and belief which serve as a just reproach to the one-sidedness of the Western tradition.

Thus, we need as clear as possible an understanding of both aspects of our theology of the Spirit: of the Spirit's part in a unified conception of God's action and of the distinctive character of his action. For the first, I do not think that we can do better than hold to Irenaeus's straightforward characterization of God's action in the world: the Father works by means of his two hands, the Son and the Spirit. That is not as inappropriate to the "spiritual" nature of God as may appear. When you use your hands, to greet someone or to write a letter, it is *you* who are doing it. "God's right arm has gained the victory" is not mere metaphor, but a metaphor that conveys a great and important Christian truth. Our God's action is not immediate but mediated action. Immediate action would overwhelm and depersonalize, if not worse; recall the story of Moses wishing to see God's glory (Ex. 33:19–23). The incarnation provides our chief model of mediation. God's actions in Christ are sovereign and achieve their end, while they respect our createdness and personhood. But the incarnation happens through the Spirit too, and in that respect God's actions in the Spirit serve to bring about those things God purposes in Christ. In sum: all divine action, whether in creation, salvation, or final redemption is the action of God the Father; but it is all equally brought about by his two hands, the Son and the Spirit. And these hands do not act separately, like someone holding a baby in one hand and trying to bang in a nail with the other (though I fear that our talk of the Spirit might sometimes suggest that). The Spirit works through the Son, just as Jesus' ministry was empowered by the Spirit. All is the unified action of the one God, the one God of Old Testament confession, mediated in this twofold way.

How, then, do we achieve our second aim, of doing justice to the distinctions, the differences, between the Persons? Let me approach that by outlining a further complication. It is not in every way a bad thing that we do not speak much about the Spirit. It is sometimes said that the Spirit is the self-effacing Person of the Trinity. Think especially of John's Gospel, where the Spirit is sent to witness, to draw human beings to Jesus, and through him to God the Father. That "self-effacingness" is even, though in a different way, the case with Jesus in that Gospel, who is sent to do the Father's work. Compare also the apparently offensive saying recorded by Mark, and altered in other accounts: "Why do you call me good? No one is good except God alone" (Mark 10:18, NEB). Jesus indeed effaces himself so that he may point us to his Father, but he does not efface himself in the same way as the Spirit does. The Spirit's characteristic action is self-effacing, because the Spirit is the one who enables people and things to be themselves through Jesus Christ. We are called to proclaim Jesus Christ, not, or at least not in the same way, to proclaim the Spirit (and that is perhaps where some Pentecostalist emphases are wrong). The Spirit is the one who enables us to proclaim Jesus Christ and live in his way, so that there is a sense in which it is truer to say that we speak *from* than *about* the Spirit. And yet we need to know from whom we are speaking. If the Spirit is a person, then we need to identify, to mark out the being, of the kind of person with whom we have to do.

We have, then, but begun our differentiation of the three Persons of the Trinity, but need to be more specific. If we are to identify a person, to say something about specific characteristics, something more general needs to be said. And that is something Irenaeus did not really do, tending simply to place the two hands side by side. To go to the next stage, let us consider observations about the Spirit by two later theologians, beginning with Basil of Caesarea, who speaks of "the original cause of all things that are made, the Father; . . . the creative cause, the Son; . . .the perfecting cause, the Spirit."[7] John Calvin is remarkably similar: "To the Father is attributed the beginning of activity, and the fountain and well-spring of all things; to the Son, wisdom, counsel and the ordered disposition of all things; but to the Spirit is assigned the power and efficacy of that activity."[8] It is Basil who makes, I think, the most important point. To say that the Spirit is the perfecting cause of creation is to make the Spirit the eschatological person of the

Trinity: the one who directs the creatures to where the Creator wishes them to go, to their destiny as creatures. Where the Spirit is, there do the creatures become that which God creates them to be. In our case, it means our freedom: "where the Spirit of the Lord is, there is liberty" (2 Cor. 3:17, NEB). That, we must remember, happens only through Jesus Christ, so that we are distinguishing, not separating, what the three Persons do. But the allusion to Basil takes us back toward the main track for our theme: Can we say, and in what sense, that "the Holy Spirit . . . with the Father and the Son together is worshiped and glorified"?

THE PROBLEM IN HISTORICAL CONTEXT

I have already noted that after Origen there was always a temptation in the church to rank the three Persons of the Trinity on a descending scale. This was done, let me repeat, for the best of reasons: to maintain the unity of God and to do justice to the fact that the Son and the Spirit are in certain respects subordinate to the Father. After all, the Son obeys and the Spirit is sent, subordinate functions in that they are ordered by the Father to certain forms of action. In our modern obsession with equality, we tend to think that subordination is a bad thing, but that is wrong. It is only as humble that Jesus is divine (as Barth never tired of pointing out), only as the church serves its Lord that it is truly the church. The temptation then as now was to assume that this must be wrong, and to conclude that because the Spirit is sent by the Father, he cannot be as divine as the Father. About a century after Origen, Athanasius of Alexandria wrote a series of letters in defense of the divinity of the Holy Spirit. His opponents were known as the Tropici, because they argued that when we speak of the Spirit as divine, we are using only a trope, a figure of speech. It is merely, they argued, honorific, as when one Hollywood actress tells another that her performance was divine (at least, did when language like that was modish).[9]

The Tropici, like so many of the protagonists in this struggle, were resolute defenders of the unity of God. The trouble was that they defended an abstract and unbiblical conception of divine unity. The Bible's God is rich and various in his personal being, and it was this that Athanasius was concerned to defend. Just as it was often argued that God the Son was fully divine because he brought salvation (and only God could do that), so it was argued by Athanasius that only God can make holy, so that if the Spirit makes holy, the Spirit must be God. (Calvin makes a similar point about the Spirit's work in creation: "In transfusing into all things his energy, and breathing into them essence, life, and movement, he is indeed plainly divine.")[10] This led Athanasius to attempt to do justice to the two things we have been exploring, the unity and the diversity of God's action. In his earlier arguments against the Arians he had already tried an explanation, rather different from the one Basil was to use, but complementing it: "One God, the Father, existing by himself according as He is above all [what we call "transcendent"], and appearing in the Son according as he pervades all things [immanent], and in the Spirit according as in Him He acts in all things through the Word."[11] Stressing, on the other side, the unified activity of God, he says that the Spirit is the energy of the Son, "as realizing and giving actuality to the power of God."[12] As Theodore Campbell says, there is here both equality and subordination.[13] Because the Spirit is God in action, he is equally divine; but because he is sent by the Father, he is only such *as subordinate*.

Basil faced a similar problem, and it took the form of a challenge to the very expression I have been asked to address: "who with the Father and the Son together is worshiped and glorified." He was criticized for the apparently contrary forms of benediction that he was using in worship. One form, more characteristic of the worship of the early church, was "Glory to the Father, through the Son and in the Holy Spirit." That implies the account I have been recommending: as God's action in the world is mediated through the Son and Spirit, so is our response in worship and life. In worship, we are brought to the Father by the Spirit through the Son. The other form, however, went rather differently: "Glory to the Father with the Son together with the Holy Spirit." It raised objections, because it seemed to imply an absolute equality of the three Persons, something that, as we have seen, parts of the tradition found very hard to accept. One can put the theological problem quite simply: We are enabled to worship by the Spirit; can we also be said to worship the Spirit, the one through whom we worship? Basil's opponents, this time the Pneumatomachi—

the Spirit fighters—put forward similar arguments to those of the
Tropici, concentrating on the argument that the Spirit is nowhere
explicitly called divine in scripture.[14]

Basil's great treatise on the Spirit was designed to contend that we
can, nevertheless, describe the Spirit as divine. He argues in classical
form, from the Spirit's activities. If God is given through the Spirit,
then God is what you get. He argues that the Spirit can be blas-
phemed; that he fills the universe, and can yet be present in particular places; that he intercedes; that he is described as Lord; and that
remission of sins is granted through him.

> He is called Spirit, as God is Spirit. . . . He is called holy,
> as the Father is holy and the Son is holy . . . not as being
> sanctified, but as sanctifying. He is called good, as the
> Father is good and He who was begotten of the Good is
> good. . . . He is called Paraclete, like the Only begotten,
> as He Himself says, "I will ask the Father and He will
> give you another comforter."[15]

Is it right to use both of Basil's doxologies? Why not? Insofar as the
Son and the Spirit share the Father's divinity, they are equally to be
given that which only God should receive absolutely: worship and
honor and glory. But insofar as they are his two hands, we recognize
also that they are at the same time the mediators of God the Father's
being and action. In a certain respect, we can draw a parallel with our
understanding of the doctrine of Christ. Inasmuch as Christ is both
God and man, he is at once our Lord and the one who shares our con-
dition, so that we might come before God forgiven and renewed.
Christ is both one of us and the one who is the object of our praise
and worship. The reason why we can similarly do both in the case of
the Spirit is given by the great Puritan theologian of the Holy Spirit,
John Owen: "The *divine nature* is the reason and cause of all worship;
so that it is impossible to *worship any one* person, and not worship the
whole Trinity."[16] You cannot have one without the other two, and
therefore they are worshiped together. There is, according to Owen, a
distinction of Persons according to their *operations*—what we can call
their originating and mediating activity—but not as to their being
objects of worship. "So that when by the distinct dispensation of the
Trinity, and every person, we are led to worship . . . any person, we do

herein worship the whole Trinity; and every person, by what name soever, of Father, Son or Holy Ghost, we invoke him."[17]

When we come now to ask what is the point of it all, we shall pursue the two aspects of our topic that we have met—first the being and then the action of God.

THE POINT OF IT ALL?

God's Being

The strength of Basil's argument that we worship God the Spirit with the Father and the Son is this: If the Son and the Spirit are as truly God as God the Father, then all three together are worshiped and glorified. In one respect, that is all the church is for—to praise the one who made us and has rescued us from the domain of darkness into his glorious light. The Christian life is first of all one of thanks and praise to God simply for what he eternally is, just as at our best we love our fellow human beings simply for what they are. That is in no way inconsistent or apart from saying that our worship also makes much difference in how we live our lives on earth. We need to know that it is one thing to be God, quite another to be a creature—to know what the distinction is, because that determines where are our priorities, those things we hang our lives on. And for our purposes the crucial factor is that there are no intermediates between God and the world: nothing created that we should half worship, or treat as a privileged way to God. We worship the triune God, and no other.

Here, the function of the doctrine of the Spirit is to show that God is complete in himself, as the particular kind of God we worship: the perfecting cause in respect of God's eternal being as well as of his creation. First, there is an eternal communion of love that we call the triune God. The Spirit perfects the divine communion by being the dynamic of the Father's and Son's being who they distinctly are. God's being is therefore perfect in itself, but, second, is at the same time of such a kind that its very character provides the basis of God's movement out into the world to create, to redeem, and to perfect. God is no lonely monad or self-absorbed tyrant, but one whose orientation to the other is intrinsic to his eternal being as God. God's work "outward" is an expression of what he is eternally. The Spirit, we might say, is the motor of that divine movement outward, just as the Son is its focus and model (*eikôn*). Augustine called the Spirit the bond of love between the Father and the Son, but this is in danger of leading us to think of God as a kind of self-enclosed circle. The medieval Richard of St. Victor provided the basis of a correction by making it possible to suggest that the Spirit is the focus of a love beyond the duality of Father and Son, of a love outward to the other.[18] The Spirit's distinctive inner-Trinitarian being is oriented not on inwardness, but on otherness: as perfecter both of the eternal divine communion—in which there is real distinction, *otherness*—and of God's love for the *other* in creation and redemption.

It is this God, as Father, Son, and Spirit, whom Christians worship. Thus we worship a God who is as such distinguished from every other principle of lordship or object of worship. That is the point of Basil's second doxology, "Glory to the Father with the Son together with the Holy Spirit." But we worship in a world that has numerous other objects and focuses to which to attribute absolute value. There are a number of candidates for divine status in our world, and that is where it is peculiarly like the ancient world in which Basil and his colleagues did their theology: in the words of Paul, "there are many gods and many lords" (1 Cor. 8:5). Our age has two in particular, the self and the earth—the god within and the god in nature (in the end, they come to the same thing). But there is no god within, only a mess. The self is our problem, not our solution. There is likewise no god in the earth, except the one that, having given us life, can offer us only death, not the resurrection of the dead.[19]

In sum, to ask what the doctrine of the third Person of the Trinity achieved, in its development in Basil and the other Cappadocians, is to inquire your way to the completed doctrine of the Trinity—complete at least in its confirming of the absolute distinction, begun in Irenaeus two centuries before, between the Creator on the one hand and the creation on the other. To say that there is an absolute difference in being between God and the world is to say: "Look out, up even, but not in or down, if you want to know the real source of our being and meaning. To look into the self or the earth is to put your trust in that which cannot save." The doctrine of the Trinity is the church's resource against idolatry, against worshiping anything other than the one who by the eternal Spirit raised Jesus from the dead.

God's Action

But if you ask how this is to be, then you need Basil's other doxology: through the Son and in the Spirit. There is no God within, but there is the Son who comes alongside us in mercy and judgment. There is no God in the earth, but there is the Spirit who comes, through that same Son, to transform our personal being into that which it was created for, a living sacrifice of praise and thanks to God the Father. The Pauline blessing speaks of the communion of the Holy Spirit, and I think we can take this to mean the communion with God that the Holy Spirit gives (2 Cor. 13:13). John Owen again: "And truly for sinners to have fellowship with God, the infinitely holy God, is an astonishing dispensation."[20] That is what all are offered through the Spirit now, in the present. Perhaps the great expression of this in scripture is Eph. 2: 18 (NEB): "For through [Christ] we both alike [Jew and Gentile] have access to the Father in the one Spirit." Listen also to 1 John 1:3 (NEB): "that life which we share [*koinonia*] with the Father and his Son Jesus Christ."

In one sense, that communion is an end in itself, just as the life of the triune God is quite complete without there being a world. Yet just as the Spirit is the focus of God's creation and love of the other, so the distinctive personal action of the Spirit is to prevent us from being content with that communion, but to move us to share it with the world. The mission of the Spirit, his sending by the Father through the Son, is to create communion in the church, and in so doing to prevent the church from remaining content with its own fellowship. Speaking of the Fourth Gospel's teaching on this topic, Francis Watson writes:

> The movement of the Spirit towards Jesus' followers includes them within the scope of Jesus' relation to his Father, thereby gathering them together in *koinonia* with one another. But it also has the effect of directing them outwards, turning them towards the world. The comfort that the Spirit brings is not the comfort of communal self-absorption, for it is the role of the Spirit to bear witness to Jesus in the world, and to enable Jesus' followers to do likewise (15.26–27; 16.7–11).[21]

CONCLUSION

For Basil, as we have seen, the chief work of the Spirit consists in making the church holy: hence the "Holy Spirit," whose action is, in the New Testament, often concentrated on the church. That is something we need to relearn today, and it takes us back near to where I began, with the fact that the final, eschatological book of the New Testament becomes possible through the work of the Spirit on the Lord's day. Worship, communion, the fellowship of the last days, all these are the gifts of God the Spirit as he relates his chosen people to God the Father through the one who became man and died for us. If nothing else comes out of this essay, I hope it will be a conviction that we need to recover again a sense of the church as the holy people of God, called first and last to praise his—threefold—name in all the ways that it can be done: formal worship, holy living, and the proclamation of the gospel in all the world. We shall not perform that mission unless we learn again what it is for the church to be God's distinctive and holy people in a world that for the most part seeks and worships gods and lords other than the one triune God of scripture. One of the things that recent reappropriation of our Jewish heritage is teaching us also is the importance of Torah, of God's dispensation for those who are chosen to be his holy people on earth—the people who are different because he is different. Holiness is the gift of the Spirit, and, as Calvin knew so well, the Spirit works in part through the law that God has given to be a guide to our life on earth, through the routines of worship and behavior that we learn among the people of God. The Fathers were not all that far out in concentrating on the Spirit as the one who sanctifies.

Yet there is also a weakness in the ancient account, located in its perhaps too restricted concern with sanctification. It is now fashionable to extend the Spirit's action to the created world as a whole, especially in view of our ecological worries. Although, as I have suggested, there are in that dangers of idolatry, so that we must be cautious, yet there are positive points to be made.

First, let us return to Basil: The Spirit is the one who perfects all God's creating action, and that is why Calvin, for example, is quite happy to attribute all right human action in the arts and politics to the action of the Spirit.[22] Wherever there is truth and right is done, there is indeed the perfecting Spirit. But, second, perfection is, after the Fall, or however we wish to characterize the sway of sin, death and the devil,[23] achieved only through the incarnation, life, death, and resurrection of the Son of God. Perfection comes only by salvation, and that means that things become what they are only by being brought back into right relation with God through Jesus Christ. The Spirit is the one who restores through Christ the direction of things to their proper end. And the call of the church, its mission, is to remind the world that, as the priests of nature, human beings are called to enable the world to be itself—which means to praise the one who made it. In that service, and in the gift of God the Spirit alone, is all true art and science, political and natural alike.

Finally, a brief return to the point made at the beginning about our distinctive modern situation. In many ways our world is very like that of the early church: pluralistic, hedonistic, moving perhaps toward the death of a civilization. The way in which it is different is that, as Robert Jenson has pointed out, this is the first culture to have rejected the gospel after once having, apparently, accepted it. That makes our mission all the more complex and difficult. How do you communicate the gospel in a world that is effectively inoculated against it? How do we, like the early church, outthink and outlive the decadent civilization around us? A large part of the answer lies in the one whose being and action we have been exploring, so that it seems to me both right and necessary that we should pray: "Come, Holy Spirit," come and lead us into the truth that is Jesus Christ, the only Son of the Father, full of grace and truth.

NOTES

1. The suppositions that this book is both a consummate literary product, which draws on a long tradition of language and imagery, and the product of some kind of ecstatic experience are by no means in conflict with each other. The processes of deep learning and inspiration involved are wonderfully illustrated by J. Livingston Lowes, *The Road to Xanadu* (Boston and New York: Houghton Mifflin Co., 1927).

2. "The Bible's closest approach to a definition of the divine nature, that 'God is Spirit.'" Robert W. Jenson, *Systematic Theology*, vol. 1, *The Triune God* (New York and Oxford: Oxford University Press, 1977), p. 146. That, of course, is what Hegel also thought, and might be queried in the light of another near

definition from earlier in that same chapter, that God is love (1 John 4:16).

3. "Now what has been made is a different thing from him who makes it. The breath, then, is temporal, but the Spirit is eternal." Irenaeus, *Against the Heresies,* 5.12.2. This is particularly important in view of the still-repeated canard that Irenaeus was only an "economic" Trinitarian.

4. For evidence that this may not necessarily be the case with Origen, see David Rainey, "The Argument for the Deity of the Holy Spirit according to St. Basil the Great, Bishop of Caesarea." M.Th. thesis, Vancouver School of Theology, 1991, pp. 11–13, referring especially to *De Principiis.* 1.3.7.

5. We speak, for example, of the Holy Spirit "indwelling" believers, but what sense does it make unless we relate this action to that of the Father and the Son?

6. Which we can, as a result, call with equal validity mother and daughter, in contradiction of scripture, than which we presume to know better.

7. Basil of Caesarea, *On the Holy Spirit,* 15.36 and 38.

8. John Calvin, *Institutes of the Christian Religion,* Library of Christian Classics, ed. John T. McNeill, trans. Ford Lewis Battles (Philadelphia: Westminster Press, 1960), 1.13.18. Compare John Owen, *Of Communion with God the Father, Son and Holy Ghost, Each Person Distinctly, in Love, Grace and Consolation; or, The Saints' Fellowship with the Father, Son and Holy Ghost Unfolded,* vol. 2, *The Works of John Owen,* ed. William H. Goold (London: Banner of Truth, 1966), p. 16: "The father doeth it by the way of *original authority*; the son by the Way of communicating from a *purchased treasury*; the Holy Spirit by the way of *immediate efficacy.*"

9. The arguments of this group bear a remarkable similarity to some proponents of today's "metaphorical theology," arguing as they do on the basis of a unity of God underlying the apparent plurality that one can in effect project onto deity such attributes as appear to suit the needs of the day.

10. Calvin, *Institutes,* 1.13.14.

11. Athanasius, *Orations against the Arians,* 3.15.

12. Theodore Campbell, "The Doctrine of the Holy Spirit in the Theology of Athanasius," *Scottish Journal of Theology* 27 (1974): 408–40 (427).

13. Campbell, "Doctrine of the Holy Spirit," 429.

14. This was something of a commonplace. In his fifth Theological Oration, Gregory of Nazianzus also acknowledges that the deity of the Spirit is not clearly and explicitly taught in scripture.

15. Basil, *Holy Spirit,* 9.48.

16. Owen, *Of Communion,* Recall the word "together" in our creedal formula. Italics added.

17. Ibid., pp. 268–69. I owe this reference to Kelly Kapic.

18. Richard of St. Victor, *On the Trinity,* 3. 19–20.

19. We are today too much inclined to put our faith in politics also. Just after the present British government was elected in 1992, someone at a conference in Australia opined that there seemed to be new hope in Britain: "Tony Blair." My reply was instant, skeptical, and biblical: "Put not your trust in princes . . ." (Ps. 146:3, KJV).

20. Owen, *Of Communion,* p. 7.

21. Francis Watson, "Trinity and Community: A Reading of John 17," *International Journal of Systematic Theology* 1, no. 2 (1999): 167–83 (182). In a recent article it was argued that Britain would now be a gentler place if churches had built up their communities rather than spending their energies trying to persuade Mrs. Thatcher to change her policies. Iain Murray, "Faith Healing," *The Spectator* 9 (October 1999): 22–24.

22. Calvin, *Institutes,* 2.2.12–17. It is also noteworthy that Basil at times Platonizes the Spirit, takes him out of the realm of material creation. "Holy Spirit" is a name peculiarly appropriate to everything that is incorporeal, purely immaterial, and indivisible (9.22)—like raising Jesus from the dead? we might inquire. "Now the Spirit is not brought into intimate association with the soul by local approximation. How indeed could there be a corporeal approach to the incorporeal?" Irenaeus would, I think, conceive otherwise, as did Owen. See the final words of the passage cited in note 8.

23. See here Carl Braaten and Robert Jenson, eds., *Sin, Death and the Devil* (Grand Rapids: Wm. B. Eerdmans Publishing Co., 1999).

We Believe in the Holy Spirit, Who Has Spoken through the Prophets

Cynthia M. Campbell

I begin my reflection on "the Holy Spirit, who has spoken through the prophets," with three memories.

Memory 1: It was a warm fall afternoon, not unlike today. Home from high school, I was sitting on my bed reading the farewell discourse in John's Gospel. I do not remember why I was doing this, but I do remember coming to a particular point where almost audibly I could hear Jesus saying, "I am the vine, you are the branches. . . . Peace I give to you. . . . In my Father's house are many rooms; if it were not so, would I have told you that I go to prepare a place for you?" Even though I knew there was no one in the room with me, there was at that moment a profound sense that these were Jesus' words.

Memory 2: Five or six years later I found myself in a classroom at the Harvard Divinity School, in George MacRae's "Gospel of John" course. Seldom before or since have I ever heard anyone lecture as brilliantly as George MacRae. As we moved through that course it became clearer and clearer to me that the chance was remote that Jesus had actually said much of anything in John's Gospel. Although my mind was not especially troubled by this, I confess that I felt a certain loss in my heart. But even as I experienced that loss, MacRae began to open up the intricate patterns of language and layers of meaning throughout John's Gospel. I fell in love with this language in a new way: Where did he come from? Where is he going? What is the way? Who sees? Who is blind? Who is alive? Who is born anew? And where did he come from, anyway?

Memory 3: Nearly fifteen years later, on a cold November day, I found myself at a grave site in a small town in north central Kansas. Not many people were there—a few family and friends, the funeral director, and me. This must have been my tenth or eleventh funeral in the first four months of my pastorate in Salina. After I finished the brief committal service, we all stood around the open grave for several minutes, remarking to each other that there was no moisture in the soil, even at the bottom of the grave. The wheat crop had been meager that summer, and now it was going to be very difficult to plant a new crop. Yet, in that moment, the words from the committal service that I had just recited came back to me. They were truth for both the living and the dead: *"In my Father's house there are many rooms. If it were not so, would I have told you that I go to prepare a place for you? . . . Let not your hearts be troubled . . . do not be afraid."*

Three memories, three stages along the way, and at each point I believe I was in the accompanying presence of the Holy Spirit—what our tradition calls the "inner illumination" of the Spirit. It was the Spirit who made those words, in different times and in different ways, the word of God. The original form of the creed that we call the Nicene Creed came to an abrupt end, stating simply, "We believe in the Holy Spirit." It is as if all of the Council's theological energies had been expended on getting it right about Jesus Christ, "begotten, not made, of one being with the Father." An *iota* of difference made all the difference in the world—*homoousias,* not *homoiousias* (the *same* being, not *like* being)! It was not until decades later that the third article of the Creed was completed, and the Holy Spirit was identified as the one who spoke through the prophets. In this phrase the Creed links the Holy Spirit to the scriptures and the scriptures to the Spirit, all within the activity of the triune God.

Linking the Spirit and the scriptures seems obvious, perhaps the most obvious thing that one could say about the Spirit's activity. The first testament is replete with men and women who are inspired by the Spirit, indwelt with the Spirit, to speak a word from the Lord. The writings of the earliest Christian communities are filled with stories of proclamation, healing, and witnessing unto death, all in the power of the Spirit and by the Spirit's leadership. The church believed that God was continuing to do what God had always done—to speak, to communicate, and thus to give life.

There are numerous ways that I could approach our topic, "Who has spoken through the prophets." It would be easy to get sidetracked by exploring intriguing questions such as the inspiration of scripture, or the various theories of how scripture is inspired, or the authority of scripture in the life of the church. However, I want to concentrate on the *work* of the Spirit, and in particular on the Spirit's relation to scripture and to speaking. First, I will direct our attention to the astounding claim that God speaks at all to anyone, let alone to us. Second, I will remind us of the distinctively Reformed discussion of the "inner illumination of the Spirit" as necessary for a reading of scripture that produces saving faith. Finally, I want to address the problems of prophets.

GOD SPEAKS

It begins at the beginning: "Then God said 'Let there be light'; and there was light." It could have happened in any number of ways, one supposes, but according to the biblical imagination, the act of creation was verbal and audible. In the beginning was the word—not the picture, not the music, not the energy, not even the thought, but the word—a speech act. The relationship between God and humankind is from the beginning conversational. The Lord God strolls through the garden at the time of the evening breeze looking for the companion creatures. Because the Lord God cannot find them, he calls out, "Where are you?" and thus brings them out of hiding. While it is true that Elijah finally came face to face with God in the sound of sheer silence, for the most part God does a lot of talking in the Bible. God delivers construction plans to Noah, birth announcements to Abraham and Sarah, and marching orders to Moses and the Hebrew slaves. The third book of Moses, Leviticus, moves forward with the repeated phase "The LORD spoke to Moses, saying . . . ." Later, of course, come the prophets, whose vocation—whose blessing and curse—was to speak the word of the Lord, to bring good news to the poor and bad news to the proud. Jesus came with a healing touch and did many deeds of power, but it was as teacher, Rabbi, speaker, that he was most well known.

It would be easy to say that this speaking God does is merely the most obvious of anthropomorphisms, depicting God after the image and likeness of the human. The resemblance between God and the human is found not in our capacity for procreation but rather in our capacity for locution. Biblical religion, the skeptic might say, is not a fertility cult, but a word cult. People of biblical faith stand such skepticism on its head, however. God speaks to us because we are creatures who speak and listen. God communicates to humanity with words because that is the way that God created us to communicate. God is a talking God because we are talking creatures. John Calvin describes this as one of the ways in which God "accommodates" and "condescends" to humankind. Out of the great love that God has for us, says Calvin, the infinite, eternal, and sovereign One bends down to us, using the means by which we communicate in order to communicate with us. God "provides for our weakness in that he prefers to address us in human fashion through interpreters in order to draw us to himself, rather than to thunder at us and drive us away."[1] Isn't that a great line . . . to communicate with us through interpreters rather than to thunder at us and frighten us to death?

Just as God has chosen to speak to us in words because we are verbal creatures, so God is also present to us in bread, wine, and water because we are creatures who depend on bread, wine, and water for life itself. Calvin again says, "Here our merciful Lord, according to his infinite kindness, so tempers himself to our capacity that, since we are creatures to always creep on the ground, cleave to the flesh, and do not think about or even conceive of anything spiritual, God condescends to lead us to himself by these earthly elements, and to set before us in the flesh a mirror of spiritual blessings."[2] All of this, Calvin argues, is the work of the Holy Spirit.

We could explore many aspects of this notion that God is a talking God, that God speaks when relating to God's human creatures. I wish to draw particular attention to the public character of this divine-human relationship. Conversation—speaking and listening—is not the act of an individual alone. Conversation is public. It occurs not within the solitary individual, but between persons in relationship. (It is true that many of us "talk to ourselves" from time to time, but we understand this is only analogous to real conversation.) Thus, God does not relate only to me in the private depths of my soul. God speaks to *us,* the people of Israel, the people of God, all the families of the earth. This conversational relationship between God and humanity occurs in public.

To say that God is a talking God also implies that God has created humans to talk back. The Bible makes it abundantly clear that God did not make humans simply to listen and obey. God expects response, and even seems open to argument and debate. In a wonderful scene in Exodus 32, Moses argues God out of destroying the people for making and worshiping a golden calf. Moses seems to chide God by asking if the Lord wants it said that he saved the people only to destroy them? What kind of God would that be? What would the Egyptians say? So, on divine second thought, God changes God's mind . . . because Moses talked back!

God speaks and the universe takes shape, life emerges, creation is born. God speaks and calls people to be the Lord's own, chosen ones to hear God's word and keep it. God speaks and saves, calling by name and making people God's own. God speaks and invites men, women, children, and young people into new relationships. Throughout the divine-human relationship, God accommodates Godself to our way of being through language. The Reformed tradition affirms that it is through this same word spoken, written, and proclaimed that God comes to us today.

THE TEXT AND THE TEACHER

In choral music, certain pieces are called "old chestnuts," or "warhorses." These quaint terms often refer to anthems or solos that have been around so long and have been performed so often that we may be embarrassed to admit that we still like them. Two pieces based on the same scriptural text fit this description well, and it happens that they both relate to our topic. Handel set it as a soprano solo—"How beautiful are the feet of them that preach the gospel of peace." Mendelssohn composed it as a choir anthem—"How lovely are the messengers." If you remember these pieces, hearing them in your mind's ear, then you know that they "dance," for they are both in three-quarter time. It is impossible for me to sing these lilting phrases without a smile on my face as well as in my voice, because the word of God is sweeter than honey.

The Reformed tradition's way of being Christian is rightly described as word-based, or even word-intoxicated. Yet our understanding of how scripture functions in the life of faith and in the church is far removed from the simple biblicism, "The Bible says it, I believe it, and that settles it." Beginning with Calvin, Reformed Christians have argued that the Bible is the word of God for us by the power of the Holy Spirit. It is the Spirit that makes the words dance. This conviction comes into focus for Calvin when he asks how we know that the scriptures are authoritative. The authority of scripture, Calvin argues, does not come from the church. Even though the church determines the canon of scripture, the church is not the source of scripture's authority. But neither can we prove the authority of scripture by virtue of reason, logical argument, or even external verification.

Calvin argues that the authority of scripture for Christian faith derives from the fact that God, in person, speaks it. The tense of the verb is quite important. We cannot know that God *spoke* through the scriptures unless we experience the reality that God *speaks* through the scriptures. God speaks to us now in what Calvin calls the "inner testimony of the Holy Spirit." Calvin writes, "The same Spirit, therefore, who has spoken through the mouths of the prophets must penetrate into our hearts to persuade us that they faithfully proclaimed what had been divinely commanded."[3] Those who are led by the Spirit—the "inner teacher"[4] by whose effort the promise of salvation penetrates our minds—will become convinced that the Bible is the very word of God.

Calvin's notion of the inner illumination of the Spirit is picked up by the confessions of the Reformed era and is particularly prominent in the first chapter of the Westminster Confession of Faith, "Of the Holy Scripture." Although Westminster is clear that "The whole counsel of God, concerning all things necessary for his own glory, [human] salvation, faith, and life, is either expressly set down in Scripture, or by good and necessary consequence may be deduced from Scripture." But the confession goes on to say, "Nevertheless we acknowledge the inward illumination of the Spirit of God to be necessary for the saving understanding of such things as are revealed in the Word."[5]

The inner illumination of the Spirit is necessary for us to see words as *the word*. According to this view, the Spirit not only *spoke* through the prophets, the Spirit *speaks* to us today. Thus, the Spirit's role in the inspiration of scripture is not confined to the past. The Holy Spirit is necessary for scripture to be the word of God for us *now*. It is the Spirit who teaches us the meaning of the scriptures. The Holy Spirit guides us by illuminating the path, thus disclosing God in our place and our time.

The Reformed tradition assumes that the regular means by which this disclosure occurs is the preaching and the hearing of the word in corporate worship. The Second Helvetic Confession puts this quite boldly (and, I must admit, in terrifying words): "The Preaching of the Word of God is the Word of God. Wherefore when this Word of God is now preached in the church by preachers lawfully called, we believe that the very Word of God is proclaimed, and received by the faithful; and that neither any other Word of God is to be invented nor is to be expected from heaven."[6] The Holy Spirit works through the education, training, continuing studying, and piety of the preacher, in company with the attentive congregation of the faithful, to make the word of God come alive today.

The Confession of 1967 makes the same point in more contemporary form: "God's word is spoken [note the verb tense again] to [the] church today where the Scriptures are faithfully preached and attentively read in dependence on the illumination of the Holy Spirit and with a readiness to receive their truth and direction."[7] It is precisely this conviction that stands behind the occasionally overlooked but distinctively Reformed liturgical tradition of the prayer for illumination. This prayer is our explicit recognition that, apart from the Holy Spirit's presence and work, we cannot hear God's word. The prayer does *not* belong immediately prior to the sermon, but rather prior to the reading of scripture, because it is the Spirit's presence in the word read as well as the word proclaimed that makes all of it become the word of God. The congregation, as well as the preacher, looks expectantly to the Spirit.

THE PROBLEM WITH PROPHETS

"We believe in the Holy Spirit, . . . who has spoken through the prophets." Up to this point we have focused our attention on the verb "spoke." We have considered the claim that God is in the self-communication business. We have reminded ourselves of our distinctively Reformed way of understanding the role of the Spirit in the reading, interpreting, and hearing of the word. I now invite us to turn to the end of the phrase: ". . . through the prophets."

In the context of the Creed, the reference to "prophets" is a reference to the whole of the scriptures. The word "prophets" refers broadly to all who received divine inspiration, and particularly to those who wrote it down. Yet, although the meaning of the creedal phrase has to do with the scriptures, "prophets" has a broader meaning. Prophets include, at least by implication, the broader phenomenon of those who speak up and speak out in the name of God to the people of God.

Prophets make Reformed Christians uncomfortable. Our problem is less the message than the medium. The prophetic voice has a way of being disruptive and challenging, and is as difficult when the news is good as when it is bad. The problem with prophets is that they speak a word of the Lord from beyond our immediate confines. They bring a message that challenges our current operating assumptions. In modern management jargon, they speak "outside the box." Thus, the word of grace is as hard for us as the word of judgment.

One of our problems with prophets is the difficulty in recognizing that they are prophets while they are alive. In identifying prophets, only hindsight is twenty-twenty. Martin Luther King Jr. will stand out as one of the great prophets of the twentieth century. Can you recall how difficult it was for Americans to hear him? He appeared threatening to many whites, an outsider who came into tranquil communities to stir up trouble. He angered some black leaders who wanted to go slow, not rock the boat too hard. He angered other black leaders who thought that nonviolence was weak and that the black community needed power, not prayer. Do you remember? Many people spoke out during the civil rights struggle, and it was often hard to know who was right, who spoke the truth, who brought a word from the Lord. Decades later we can look back and rightly hear Dr. King's words as carrying a word from God to us—to *all* of us.

So often, we know only in retrospect what we may not know at the time, for at the time it is seldom easy to hear or discern the voice of the prophet. It is seldom easy because there are always false prophets and blind guides. Thus, the community must engage in a process of discernment. Finally, it is the people of God who must determine what is a word from God and what is not. In the Reformed tradition, we believe that the ordinary way of discernment is discussion and debate with one another in the power of the Holy Spirit.

My across-the-hall neighbor is running for Congress. He gave an address at McCormick last week, speaking about the political process and the importance of political debate in public life. I was especially intrigued when he said that it is the nature of the political process to require argument. Politics necessitates debate among diverse points of view. My neighbor acknowledged that argument can degenerate into slogans hurled back and forth. Such sloganeering accomplishes little and gives politics a bad name. But he went on to say that genuine debate is an act of hope—hope that through our debate we will arrive at new places and envision a way forward that neither side had seen before. I believe that act of hope is what we in the Reformed tradition call the work of the Spirit in the life of the community, whether the community is ecclesial or secular.

It is hard to hear challenging prophetic words, and it is difficult to distinguish true from false prophets. But there is yet another problem with prophets. Sometimes they are simply hard to hear amid all the voices clamoring for attention. When some voices are privileged while others find it difficult to be acknowledged, then even hearing the message of the prophets becomes a problem. One of my favorite passages from the *Book of Confessions*'s "A Brief Statement of Faith" is

> "In a broken and fearful world
> the Spirit gives us courage . . .
>   to hear the voices of peoples long silenced."[8]

It was my great privilege to serve on the committee that produced the final text of the Brief Statement of Faith. As we reviewed the "In a broken and fearful world the Spirit gives us courage . . ." section, Bill Keesecker pressed for the inclusion of the phrase "to pray without ceasing." Once we started tinkering with the section, many other things that the Spirit gives us courage to do appeared as candidates for inclusion. In the midst of our discussion, Henry Fawcett of Dubuque Theological Seminary told us a story:

Presbyterian missionaries came to his home village in Alaska in the nineteenth century. Many people were converted, including members of his family. Henry's grandfather was a tribal leader who became a Christian. The missionaries taught that Christian faith meant doing away with old beliefs, rituals, idols, and community traditions. Being a Christian required getting rid of all the trappings of ancestral faith, taking new names, and adopting modern, Western ways. The new believers were asked to destroy many things as an act of faith, including drums and ceremonial blankets.

Many decades later, when his father died, Henry Fawcett returned to his family home in order to close the house and dispose of the property. As he was rummaging through the attic, he discovered a trunk that he had never seen before. At the very bottom of the trunk, under layers of ordinary household goods, he found one of his grandfather's ceremonial blankets. "I took the blanket out and held it," Henry said, "and it was as though I could hear my grandfather speaking to me. In no way do I regret the decision to follow Christ, but I do regret that I could never hear my grandfather speak in his own voice."

One of the great gifts and real challenges of our time is that so many people have discovered their voices and realized that they have something to say. Sometimes we feel inundated by too many voices, too many points of view. It may all become so frustrating that attempts to honor the voices and their concerns are dismissed as some sort of political correctness. The faces and voices of church leaders and theologians have changed dramatically since the 1960s. Women, persons of color, theologians, and church leaders from Africa, Asia, and Latin America have entered a world that for centuries belonged to white, male, European and North American scholars and leaders. The change is revolutionary, for we know that social and cultural location is a critical factor in discerning and communicating the word of God.

The language of the Brief Statement does more than call us to expand the range of conversation partners, however. It calls us to recognize that some voices have not simply been silent: others have silenced them. Some voices have been excluded from the conversation. They have been intentionally overlooked, ignored, rejected, and silenced. The force of that realization drives in two directions. Some of us need to consider whether our own voices have been or are being silenced, to ask whether we have been reluctant to speak, unwilling to claim a voice. Some of us need to consider whether we have kept others out of the conversation, drowning out their voices with our clever words and decisive convictions. Some of us may have been in both camps, at different times. Hearing the voices of people long silenced—our own voices and the voices of others—requires courage. We affirm that the courage we need is itself a work of the Spirit.

"We believe in the Holy Spirit, the Lord, the giver of life, . . . who has spoken through the prophets." I have attempted to highlight three aspects of that affirmation.

First, the frankly audacious claim that God speaks, that God communicates to us in ways we can and do understand. God's self-expression, this gift of God's self-communication, is as great a miracle as the creation itself. It stands as a sign that we are not alone, that we are creatures who are addressed by God and who are invited to talk back. Second, we in the Reformed tradition affirm that God not only spoke in times past, but also that God speaks now, to us. Indeed, only in and through God's speaking Spirit do the words of the past come alive, so that the words of preachers and presbytery debates may become the word of God for us. And finally, we affirm that the Spirit speaks through prophets—those voices from the margin that speak truth to power, voices that confront and comfort, voices long silenced that erupt into speech and song.

One of my favorite hymns traces its roots to the *Yigdal,* a formulation of the Jewish faith by Moses ben Maimon, known as Maimonedes. The text in *The Presbyterian Hymnal* (Hymn 488) is a translation of the early-fifteenth-century metric version of the *Yigdal.* The second stanza captures what our discussion has been about:

> Your Spirit still flows free,
> High surging where it will;
> In prophet's word You spoke of old
> And You speak still.

NOTES

1. John Calvin, *Institutes of the Christian Religion,* Library of Christian Classics, ed. John T. McNeill, trans. Ford Lewis Battles (Philadelphia: Westminster Press, 1960), 3.2.36.
2. Ibid., 4.14.3.
3. Ibid., 1.7.4.
4. Ibid., 2.2.20.
5. "The Westminster Confession of Faith," *The Book of Confessions: Study Edition* (Louisville: Geneva Press, 1999), 6.006.
6. "The Second Helvetic Confession," *The Book of Confessions: Study Edition,* 5.004.
7. "The Confession of 1967," *The Book of Confessions: Study Edition,* 9.30.
8. "A Brief Statement of Faith," *The Book of Confessions: Study Edition,* 10.4, lines 65, 66, and 70.

We Believe in One Holy Catholic and Apostolic Church*

Miroslav Volf

The third article of the Christian creedal tradition consistently pairs the Holy Spirit and the church. The relationship between the Spirit and the church is an essential ecclesiological theme. Ecclesiologies that develop from the doctrine of the Spirit remain rare even as "spirituality" grows more and more fashionable. While "spirituality" is the theme of many popular books these days, their value depends on what one means by "spirituality." We tend to be seduced by words. For instance, "religion" seems like such a good word, and yet we must be wary of it. Like many other words—perhaps more than other words—"religion" is an indefinite term that refers to an ambiguous reality. As we are all aware, in the name of religion people have not only undertaken extraordinary deeds of selfless service but have perpetrated the most heinous acts of violence. Similarly, "spirituality" is ambiguous, for it refers to a wide range of attitudes and practices. Everything depends on its content. The ambiguity of such familiar, "religious" words is one reason why it is essential to reflect on the relationship between the Spirit and the church.

*The substance of this talk goes back to an essay by Miroslav Volf and Maurice Lee, "The Spirit and the Church," *The Conrad Grebel Review* (Fall 2000).

ECCLESIOLOGY, PNEUMATOLOGY, AND CHRISTOLOGY

In the tradition, we can trace the pairing of the church and the Spirit back to the early third century. According to the *Apostolic Tradition* of Hippolytus, the third question asked of candidates for Baptism was, "Do you believe in the Holy Spirit, and the Holy Church, and the resurrection of the flesh?" This connection in the creedal tradition echoes the close ties between the Holy Spirit and the church found throughout the New Testament. The account of the Spirit's coming at Pentecost paradigmatically attests that the church was born out of the womb of the Spirit. From their beginnings, throughout their history, the Christian dogmatic and theological traditions have acknowledged the Spirit as the generative force, the life-giving environment, the breathing room of the church.

Although both scripture and tradition attest to the pervasive association between Spirit and church, theologians have tended not to reflect on precisely how the two are related. This relative absence of deep exploration can be seen even in John Calvin, a theologian who cannot be blamed for neglect of the Holy Spirit. Calvin stresses that the elect are made truly one since they live together in one faith, one hope, and one love in the one Spirit of God. Yet he does not venture to explore how the Spirit of the triune God shapes the nature and the mission of the church. Calvin is not an exception, but the rule.

This lack of concentrated attention to the relationship between the Spirit and the church stands in marked contract to explorations into the relationship between Christ and the church. The church is conceived as the body of Christ, as the bride of Christ, as Christ's servant, as the redeemed community of the crucified Lord. We could continue to cite christological modes of understanding the church, all of which are natural and appropriate. All of them are rooted in the fact that the narrative of the life, death, and resurrection of Christ is foundational throughout the New Testament. As a consequence we find very early on in Christian theology the sentiment expressed well by Ignatius of Antioch, "Where Christ is there is also the church."

But where does this concentration on the relation between Christ and church leave the Spirit? Does the Holy Spirit come only after the church has already been constructed independently, with christological material alone? Does the Holy Spirit play only a secondary role as the life-infusing and invigorating breath of the ecclesial body? Actually, that is a recurring image. Just as, according to Genesis, God created human beings by fashioning them from the earth and then breathing life into their souls, so the church was created by establishing its structure and then bringing it to life by the wind of the Spirit. There is some truth in that, but it is not the whole truth.

One reason why the tradition has not developed the pneumatological side of ecclesiology is a certain elusiveness of the Holy Spirit. This is an old, familiar pneumatological theme. Some of the early church fathers even speak of elusiveness as a constitutive feature of the Holy Spirit, who always withdraws from the picture, pointing to something else and someone else rather than putting himself in the forefront.

Talk about the Holy Spirit is often filtered christologically. We identify who the Spirit is and what the Spirit does by pointing to Christ. Except for being a source of life and power, the Spirit would then seem theologically irrelevant and ecclesiologically redundant. But this impression is false. We must retrieve the central importance of the Holy Spirit for our ecclesiology and our practice of church life. Though our knowledge of the Spirit is filtered christologically, the being and the activity of the Spirit are not simply determined in one direction by Christ. Indeed, Gospels research during the past several decades has resulted in the widespread conviction that Jesus' identity and mission were fundamentally shaped by the Spirit. Even if one does not find an exclusive Spirit Christology persuasive (and I certainly do not), it seems clear that the New Testament writers believed that Jesus was Christ because he was anointed by the Spirit.

If we take this insight of biblical scholarship seriously, then we have a threefold relationship that we have to incorporate into all of our talk about the church. The relationship between the Spirit and the church, the relationship between Christ and the church, and the complex relationship between the Spirit and Christ are all integral to the church's life. None of this is simple. The relationship between the Spirit and Christ is itself a dual one, for Christ both gives the Spirit and is the bearer of the Spirit.

REIGN OF GOD, PEOPLE OF GOD

How should we express the relationships among Christ, the Holy Spirit, and the church? I will build on some of the work of the Catholic theologian Herbert Mühlen, who attempted to develop an ecclesiology that does not build only on Christ as the giver of the Spirit or only on Christ as the receiver of the Spirit, but on both together. Mühlen defined the church as the continuation of Christ's anointing by the Spirit, the very anointing by which Jesus of Nazareth is and was the Messiah of God. Mühlen's is neither a simply incarnational understanding nor a simply pneumatic understanding, but rather a continuation of the anointing in which Jesus carried out his own ministry. I think this is an excellent way to think of the relationship between Spirit and the church, and so I will try to develop Mühlen's thesis in a somewhat more Protestant fashion. First I will talk about the relationship between the Spirit and Christ, and then I will talk about the identity and the mission of the church.

Jesus of Nazareth's consciousness of the power of God's Spirit at work in him was integral to his messianic identity and mission. I know that this is a contested claim, but I will simply let it stand. Some of you may wish to challenge me, and that may be a matter for further discussion. But if this is true, then two key questions arise for our purposes here. First, what concrete content did the Spirit give to Jesus' proclamation and enactment of God's reign? Second, how is the church related to Jesus' proclamation and enactment of God's reign? I want to address the second question first, and then come back to the first.

What is the relationship between Jesus' proclamation of the kingdom of God and the church? When I was growing up theologically, my revered teacher Jürgen Moltmann tended to downplay the significance of the church and highlight the significance of the kingdom of God. It is not the church, but the kingdom of God that is fundamental, he argued. On the whole, he is right, though his stress on the kingdom seems one-sided. For the church is not an optional extra in relation to the kingdom, but an integral part of it. We can see this very clearly in the life of Jesus.

Contemporary scholarship seems agreed that ecclesiological passages in the Gospels, such as Matthew 16:18, do not go back to Jesus himself. Strictly speaking, Jesus did not found the church. Does it therefore follow, as some scholars have argued, that the emergence of the church had little or nothing to do with the original mission of Jesus? Or can it even be said that Jesus' eschatological self-understanding is incompatible with the idea of the church? The German scholar Gerhard Lohfink has suggested that behind disjunction between the mission of Jesus and the emergence of the church lies a dichotomy between the reign of God and the people of God. Such a dichotomy between God's reign and God's people is clearly and certainly false. The reign of God is quite unthinkable without the people of God among whom it becomes a concrete reality. In Jesus' ministry the indissoluble bond between the reign of God and the people of God is most clearly manifest in the calling of the Twelve. The disciples symbolized and enacted the incipient gathering of Israel's twelve tribes as the eschatological people of God. Rather than being an alternative to the people of God, the reign of God entails the coming and final presence of God with God's people, the reconstitution of the people as unforsakably God's.

The claim that I want to make about the integral connection between the reign of God and the people of God, or the church, comes partly out of my own experience. In the preface to my book *After Our Likeness* I wrote about my experiences of growing up in a Communist country. I was the only kid in a school of three thousand who was a professing Christian. Moreover, I was part of a small, struggling minority of Protestants, and so lacked even the cultural legitimacy of the Catholic or Orthodox churches. As I reflect back on those times, it is clear to me that our church would have suffocated, would not have continued to live, if it did not look to something much greater than itself. If it had not had its windows opened to the kingdom of God, it would have withered like a plant that lacked the sustenance of water and sun. On the other hand, it is clear to me that the message of the kingdom was dependent on groups of struggling people who enacted it, who kept it alive, who proclaimed it, who made sure that the vision was there for people to hear and see.

In a sense, then, I see a dialectical relationship between the reign of God and the church of God. That is why I think the church is so very important. My remarks about the relationship of Jesus and the Spirit are meant to underscore that the church is significant in Jesus' ministry, and therefore is part and parcel of the Spirit's movement.

The second point I want to make concerns the concrete content that the Spirit gave to the ministry of Jesus. Jesus announced and demonstrated the reign of God among the people of God in a variety of concrete modes: forgiveness offered to sinners, fellowship that welcomed the outcast, care for the physically needy, and more. Central to Jesus' work of the reign of God was the making whole of bodies, persons, and relationships. Jesus' immediate predecessor, John the Baptist, was a preacher of judgment. In contrast, the most striking feature of Jesus' words and actions was the expression of unconditional grace. Jesus proclaimed and lived the free, noncoercive, unbrokered outreach of God to restore God's people to fullness of life. The power of such grace is the power of restoration to wholeness and to community. The power of grace is power that gives freedom, that opens up a space in which the unconditional outreach of God can be extended, witnessed, experienced, and accepted . . . or perhaps even rejected. The Spirit with whom Jesus was anointed and who empowered Jesus' mission is the Spirit who constitutes precisely that freedom. In the relationships established between Jesus and those whom he encountered, as well as in Jesus' own joy in the works and words given to him by the Father, room was made for the interplay of divine initiative and human response. The grace that both creates and fills this space of freedom is marked by at least two features that give it particular shape.

First, unconditional grace is not cheap grace. Forgiveness, rightly understood, does not ignore evil. Rather, forgiveness always includes naming the wrong that is being forgiven. Forgiveness affirms the assumptions and requirements of justice in the very movement of transcending them. This important claim may seem somewhat complicated, but it can be made quite simply. My teacher and then-colleague at Fuller Seminary, Lewis Smedes, put it this way: to forgive is to blame. You would certainly know that this is the case if you were forgiven by someone you did not know for something you had not done. "What do you mean you forgive me?" you might say. "I've never seen you in my life! How could I have done you anything wrong!" Obviously forgiveness entails the recognition by the forgiver that wrong was done. That kind of blame is a crucial, structural feature of forgiveness. It is precisely the characteristic feature of blame that distinguishes the grace of forgiveness from all vague notions of tolerance and acceptance. Grace is not acceptance; grace is acceptance plus nonacceptance. Because grace is acceptance in spite of the unacceptable, grace recognizes the unacceptable and so entails judgment. The forgiveness that Jesus offered to persons entails precisely this blame, and therefore is forgiveness that affirms justice. Similarly, fellowship that goes beyond mere togetherness to embrace peace and well-being among people does not turn a blind eye to inequalities and injustices. Instead, it emerges from the dynamic of community in which barriers of economic status, gender identity, and religious purity are torn down, and in which hierarchies that replicate the world's power relationships are subverted. Finally, care for the body presupposes a robust notion of bodily well-being. This means recognizing and rejecting forms of physical entrapment—suffering, sickness, possession, and death—all of the things that restrict and endanger creaturely life.

I repeat: The unconditional grace mediated by Jesus was not vague tolerance, a structural feature of contemporary society. The grace of the Lord Jesus Christ is not merely the commitment to include rather than keep out, for grace goes hand in hand with a vision of the good life that involves substantive values and determinative practices. Clearly, unconditional grace is not cheap grace.

The second feature I want to emphasize is that Jesus' offer of grace was not directed to isolated individuals. Grace was a social reality. Jesus proclaimed that his announcement and enactment of God's reign was the fulfillment of prophetic promises that God's Spirit-endowed servant would bring forth justice to the nations, preach good news to the oppressed, bind up the brokenhearted, provide for those who mourn, proclaim liberty to the captives, and announce the year of the Lord's favor. Jesus' mission was inescapably and deeply social, even political, although not in the usual sense. By announcing that the true and ultimate kingdom was present in his person through the offer of grace, Jesus subverted the defensive strategies of established authorities that enforced stability through subjugation. That is what churches and pastors and professors are called to do: to subvert the established authority that coercively reinforces stability. None of this is for the sake of subversion, but because the worldly modes of enforcement of stability diminish, injure, and even kill people. By insisting that noncoercion is appropriate to the scripture's construal of God's reign, Jesus subverted the offensive nationalist agendas that advocated victory through violence.

Jesus was well aware that his message and his actions were profoundly incompatible with ruling and revolutionary programs alike. He also knew that this incompatibility marked out a path of suffering and death that was bound up with his messianic task. It is important to realize that the way Jesus presented his claim and his message, both to individual persons and to larger social networks, involved a complex interplay of hiddenness and openness. His teaching and his acts of power were certainly public, aimed at diverse groups of people and accessible to all. Yet Jesus did not try to impart a particular title or image to represent his identity, such as messiah or healer. Why did he not do that? My guess is that he knew that such terms could be torn loose from their moorings in the specificity of his mission, and thus he and his mission would have been misunderstood and misrepresented. Thus, hiddenness served the purpose of preserving Jesus' particular identity and ensured that the message could be heard and accepted in its full integrity. (As I will say later, the same dynamic should characterize the church today.)

My brief exploration of the relation between Jesus, the Spirit, and the communities of God's people suggests the following picture: Because the reign of God is unthinkable without the people of God, the gathering of communities was inseparable from Jesus' earthly mission, carried out in the power of the Spirit. Moreover, participation in the mission of Jesus was integral to the identity of the communities that were formed in his name. Remember that Jesus sent people in the power of the Spirit to continue his own mission. Called and gathered around Jesus, these messianic communities were loyal to Jesus and his vision. They were also sent by Jesus and endowed with the same Spirit that rested on Jesus, so that they could carry on Jesus' mission to proclaim God's reign as the power of unconditional grace to make persons, relationships, and bodies whole.

This basic structure of the relation between Jesus, the Spirit, and the community evident in the ministry of Jesus was affirmed and theologically developed by the Gospel writers. This can be seen clearly in Luke-Acts. Jesus' baptism and anointing by the Spirit marked the start of his mission. Following the climax of that mission in resurrection and ascension, the same Spirit was poured out on Jesus' disciples. This

Spirit is the one through whom, according to the prophecy of Joel, all God's people will be gathered and empowered to speak God's word and announce God's reign. Similarly, John's Gospel commences Jesus' ministry by the descent of the Holy Spirit, who remained with Jesus throughout. After his death, resurrection, and exaltation, Jesus breathed this same Spirit on the disciples as he sent them into the world, just as he had been sent by the Father.

Clearly, Luke and John believed that the emergence of the church was bound up with the risen Christ's sending of the Spirit, who anointed disciples to continue the mission of Jesus. This complex of theological affirmations concerning the relation between Christ and the Spirit and the church on the part of the evangelists builds on the remembered practice and self-consciousness of Jesus. This is well summarized by Raniero Cantalamessa's metaphorical claim that the last breath of Jesus on the cross is the first breath of the church. This relationship between the Spirit and the church can also be summed up well in the claim by another Catholic scholar, Mühlen, that the church is a continuation of Christ's anointing by the Spirit.

In the remainder of this essay I will explore the implications of this claim for the mission of the church. There is insufficient time to explore the identity of the church as a community gathered in diversity, gifted for ministry, and united in love—the community that images the holy Trinity. Therefore, we must proceed directly to the mission of the church.

THE MISSION OF THE CHURCH:
REBIRTH OF PERSONS

In the power of the Spirit, Jesus announced and enacted the reign of God. In the power of the Spirit, which the risen Christ poured out on them, the disciples continued his mission in the world. This way of defining the nature of the church suggests a close relationship between the identity of the church and the mission of the church. This close relationship between the identity of the church and the mission of the church is a point that I want to underscore. If the triune God whom the church should image is engaged with a world gone awry, then it is integral to the nature of the church to be so engaged. I want to explore briefly *how* the church is to be engaged in mission. My comments come in three parts: first, the rebirth of persons; second, the reconciliation of people; and third, the care of bodies.

First, the rebirth of persons, for the church is called to proclaim that in the Holy Spirit, God seeks to pour God's own love into the hearts of those who are weak, who are sinners, who are enemies to God and one another. At the cross we see that the reach of God's love cannot be limited or confounded by ungodliness. As God lets the sun shine on just and unjust alike, so God bestows grace on all. God's commitment to each human being is irrevocable, and God's covenant is indestructible. Nothing can place a person outside the scope of God's love, and so the offer of forgiveness is universal. Of course, God's forgiveness entails blame. Far from treating human sin as if it were not present, in the act of forgiveness God names deception as deception, injustice as injustice, violence as violence. The "good news" is not that human sin does not matter. The good news is that the reality of the most heinous sin notwithstanding, God's embrace still holds. Hence the cross of Christ.

By naming sin in the context of God's unconditional grace, the Spirit of truth frees human beings from the self-deception that is rooted in conscious or unconscious efforts of self-justification. As we behold God's arms stretched out over us on the cross, by the power of the Holy Spirit we dare to look into the abyss of our own evil and recognize who we truly are—the weak, sinners, enemies, the ungodly. However, freedom from self-deception does not come simply because we know we will be embraced, or even that we have been embraced, but because the embrace of God liberates us from enslavement to evil, which so profoundly shapes us. "So if anyone is in Christ, there is a new creation: everything old has passed away; see, everything has become new!" (2 Cor. 5:17). The grace that forgives is the grace that makes new.

"New creation" is an ecclesiological reality. This suggests that the good news of God's grace to sinful humanity concerns not only our past and our present, but also our future. We are forgiven and transformed, for we have been given a new birth into a living hope through the resurrection of Jesus Christ from the dead. And this hope does not disappoint. As my colleague Serene Jones puts it, the purity of God's grace that God had poured on our imperfect, impure souls gives us assurance that not only our middle, but our end, has been folded into God's promise.

Summing up the three aspects of proclamation about the rebirth of persons—forgiveness, transformation, and hope—we can say that the church is called to proclaim the ecclesiological event of justification by grace through which God forgives, transforms, and promises to glorify sinful human beings and thus take them up into God's own Trinitarian embrace.

THE MISSION OF THE CHURCH: RECONCILIATION OF PEOPLE

We turn, second, to the reconciliation of people. At the center of God's offer of grace, which makes the sinner into a new creation, lies the act of God's self-giving in the cross of Christ. The Christian life begins in Baptism—"We have been united with him in a death like his"—and therefore reaches forward to characterize the goal of life in Christ—"We will certainly be united with him in a resurrection like his" (Rom. 6:5). Persons are identified with the death of Christ and so are portrayed as those who live by faith in the Son of God who loved them and gave himself up for them.

The reiterated celebration of the Lord's Supper enacts the very heart of the Christian life. In the Lord's Supper, Christians remember the one who gave his body for them so that they would be shaped in his image. The very being of the church is grounded in God's self-giving, and continuously constituted by God's self-giving. As the community of God's self-giving, brought to life by the self-giving presence of the Holy Spirit, the very life of the church must be modeled on God's self-giving. Divine self-giving is the form and way that God reconciled human beings to himself. The church is the community that knows God's reconciling love, and since the church's mission is the face of its identity turned toward the world, the church must engage in the ministry of reconciliation.

The church has tended to understand its ministry of reconciliation as the call of individual persons to be reconciled with God. Reconciliation in this vision has theological and personal meaning, but lacks a social meaning. In recent decades, however, Christian social engagement has often been characterized by the twin categories of liberation and justice. I think that the special prominence accorded to the themes of liberation and justice has been, at least, one-sided, and probably mistaken. The one-sided emphasis on these themes may have been a necessary correction, but it is mistaken, nonetheless. I realize that this is a controversial claim. But since this is a central assertion of my book *Exclusion and Embrace,* and since much of my work has been centered around it, I may as well say it outright.

In my view, the stress on liberation is clearly inadequate as a reading of the scriptures, and also inadequate as a reading of social realities and of ways to address social problems. My objection to the liberationist perspective is not merely theoretical, for it came to me as I was trying to figure out what to do theologically with the war that was raging in my own country, the former Yugoslavia. My instinct, having been reared at Moltmann's feet, was to apply "liberation" to the war in the former Yugoslavia. Since both oppression and liberation from oppression were occurring in my homeland, I used the lens of my theological patrimony to frame my perspective and focus my vision. Soon, it became obvious that *both* Croats and Serbs—and later Muslims—perceived themselves as the oppressed who were engaged in the struggle for liberation! Moreover, if I tried to be somewhat objective, it seemed that all of them had at least internally plausible reasons for making that claim. So if I had offered them standard liberation theology, I would only have provided combat gear, some new weapons to fight with. "Great," they would say, Croat and Serb and Muslim alike, "God is on the side of the oppressed—*our* side." And so the struggle would continue.

I needed a theological perspective that would recognize the depth of the evil that was being perpetrated there. But my theological perspective also had to offer the possibility of an end to the violence of mutual destruction, and—even more—the possibility of negotiation that might lead to future reconciliation. Hence my conclusion that any stress on liberation must be framed by the vision of reconciliation. Surely there are situations that cry out for an appropriate stress on immediate liberation. Yet liberation can never be seen as an end in itself, a goal independent of reconciliation. Liberation apart from reconciliation easily and almost inevitably becomes destructive.

These are social reasons for giving primacy to reconciliation. There are also important theological reasons for doing so. The social mission of the church ought to be pursued out of the heart of its own identity. Hence, we must retrieve and explicate the social meaning of divine self-giving in order to reconcile sinful humanity. Paul described the ministry of reconciliation as appealing to people to be reconciled to God. That appeal and that ministry have an inviolable social dimension, however, because reconciliation among human beings is intrinsic to the reconciliation between humans and God. At its center, not only at its periphery, reconciliation has a horizontal dimension as well as a vertical one. Reconciliation is a turning away from enmity toward real people as well as the turning away from enmity toward God. Moreover, reconciliation is a movement toward the other who was the target of enmity; hence the Pauline vision of reconciliation between Jews and Gentiles, between men and women, between slave and free. Hence also the grand vision of Colossians that in Christ "all the fullness of God was pleased to dwell," and that through Christ "God was pleased to reconcile to himself all things, whether on earth or in heaven, by making peace through the blood of his cross" (Col. 1:19–20). The ultimate goal, not only for the church but for the whole of reality, is a vision of the reconciliation of all things in the embrace of the triune God.

Reconciliation, and therefore grace, is at the center of the church's social mission. While we must never conceive of reconciliation in opposition to liberation, or grace in contrast to justice, within the dialectical relation between liberation and reconciliation, we need to give priority to reconciliation. The issue is not excluding one or the other, but where the priority lies. It is essential to underscore both the priority of reconciliation over liberation and the dialectical relationship between the two. Apart from the priority of reconciliation, the pursuit of liberation never leads to peace and love between former enemies. But without commitment to justice, the pursuit of reconciliation is perverted into the perpetuation of domination and oppression, into "pacification," one might say. Just as the proclamation of God's embrace is centered in grace that affirms justice as part of its inner makeup, so the practice of social reconciliation must include a struggle for liberation within the overarching framework of embrace.

THE MISSION OF THE CHURCH: CARE OF BODIES

As we have seen, central to Jesus' mission was the care of bodies. His programmatic sermon in Nazareth makes this plain:

> "The Spirit of the Lord is upon me,
>   because he has anointed me
>   to bring good news to the poor.
> He has sent me to proclaim release to the captives
>   and recovery of sight to the blind,
>   to let the oppressed go free,
> to proclaim the year of the Lord's favor."
>
> (Luke 4:18–19)

Attempts at spiritualizing Jesus' care for bodies abound. Consonant with his soteriology, Martin Luther, for example, consistently translated accounts of Christ's healing of human bodies into reports on how Jesus liberates the *conscience* through the forgiveness of sin. But this will clearly not do as an adequate reading of the Gospels: Jesus forgave *and* he healed. The early church, at least ideally, continued with the same kind of care for bodies. It healed the sick and it supported the poor so that "there was not a needy person among them" (Acts 4:34). The apostle Paul, too, did not only proclaim reconciliation; he also helped the poor and healed the sick.

Behind the care of bodies lies the persuasion that the rebirth of persons who live in this material world, and who with this world make up the good creation of God, cannot be complete without the redemption of their bodies. The new birth of persons through the Spirit must be seen as the beginning—the ambiguous but nonetheless real beginning—of the rebirth of the whole cosmos. Similarly, the reconciliation of people who live embodied lives will be complete only when the reconciliation of all things takes place; there can be no eschatological bliss for God's people without eschatological shalom for God's world. Hence, the care of bodies, broadly conceived, belongs properly to the mission of the church.

If we understand the mission of the church to include care for bodies, and in so doing to address the larger social and ecological issues, where does the Spirit come in? Often the work of the Spirit has been limited to the church, the gathering of people into communities, to gifting them, to uniting them, to inspiring them to proclaim the gospel, which aims in turn at further gathering. But is such a "centripetal" understanding of the work of the Spirit adequate? Even more, are the implicit ecclesiological assumptions that inform it correct—namely, that the church is only a church when gathered, but not when "scattered," and that the work of the church is therefore primarily liturgical and not "secular"? Properly understood, the church is not a "gathering" but a *community that gathers,* and ecclesial work is therefore done both when the community is "gathered" and when it is "scattered" in the world. Since to live as a Christian means to "walk in the Spirit," *all* Christian work is done in the power of the Spirit, whether it concerns the rebirth of persons, the reconciliation of people, or the care of bodies.

As the community of faith reaches into the world to touch all dimensions of its life, it will find that the Spirit of Christ at work in the community is the Spirit of life at work in the whole creation. Anointed by the Spirit, the church is sent to go where the Spirit is always already to be found preparing the way for the coming reign of God.

HIDDENNESS AND OPENNESS

I conclude by looking once more at hiddenness and openness. All aspects of the church's mission entail a complex interplay between hiddenness and openness, analogous to what we see in Jesus' ministry. The church does not seek to draw attention to itself. In the Catholic tradition, there is an image of the church as the moon, a body that has no light of its own. All of the moon's light is reflected. Similarly, the church does not seek to draw people; rather it points away from itself. The church's worship and service point to Christ as the way to the Father and, by pointing to him, point to the reign of God. This notion takes Jesus' own practice of hiddenness a step farther still. Jesus refused to identify himself or to exalt himself in ways that would have reinforced popular expectations and assumptions. Yet Jesus' words and deeds grew from the belief in his own centrality to the mission for which he had been anointed and which was meant for all of God's people. Similarly, the church sent by Christ and anointed by the Spirit should not identify itself or exalt itself in the service of self-interest. But there is more. The church must harbor no illusions about its centrality, for its anointing by the Spirit is for *Christ's* mission. The center around which the church's existence and work are organized is not itself, but *Christ,* all for the sake of making the grace of *God's* reign known.

The displacement of the church's center away from itself to Christ is absolutely crucial and central. This radical decenteredness is by no means an excuse for the church to avoid its proper agency. Rather, the church's decenteredness bestows the courage to live as a misfit in its pursuit of faithful mission in the world, the courage to be out of step with the surrounding culture's plausibility structures and social arrangements. The culture is constituted by dominant paradigms that present the church with customary social roles and conventional expectations, many of these quite detached from its mandate to proclaim and present the reign of God. To the extent that the church understands that its identity and mission are not its own, but Christ's, it will resist having its place and boundaries marked out by assumptions and presumptions that do not arise from its union with Christ in the Spirit. Thus, the church's hiddenness is not a form of withdrawal or a sectarian privatization of religious life. The church does not hide itself in blissful, insulated isolation, floating above the tangible needs and wounds, animosities and hopes, that characterize every human social context. Rather, the church's hiddenness is a form of openness. Decentered from itself and into Christ, the church is able to resist forces that would bend and shape it into just one more sociocultural institution. Decentered from itself and into Christ, the church is set free to announce and demonstrate the grace of God that changes the world. This interplay of hiddenness and openness, emerging from the church's anointing by the Spirit of Christ, frees the church from facile distortions of its identity and oppressive demands on its mission. The interplay of hiddenness and openness also sets the church free to subvert, challenge, and transform both the public vision of its own salutary future and its ways of creating that future.

One sometimes hears rhetoric that sounds like what I am saying. Such rhetoric claims that it is always right for the church to be distinct from and opposed to the culture, "resident aliens" . . . "strangers in a strange land." I must say that such rhetoric does not strike me as right either. The point is not to be in opposition—there are plenty of oppositions. The point is not to be a misfit—there are zillions of ways to be misfitted. There is no virtue in being opposed to the world or misfitted. The point of it all is to draw one's identity, and mission, from the presence of Christ and the Spirit. That center is the ground of our misfit, and thus the source of our appropriate opposition.

The church cannot be defined either by the necessity to identify with something else, or by necessity to oppose it. Thus, the one holy catholic and apostolic church transcends the classic distinction between the sect, which primarily opposes, and the church, which primarily nods its head and accommodates the established order. The point is not distance and opposition. The point is living out of one's own proper identity, which is defined by the Spirit of God that rested on Christ and in whose power the church continues to exist. The church is appropriately and faithfully public as it offers an alternative vision in which the reign of God is displayed in all aspects of life for all to see. In this way the church pursues the mission that is at the core of its own identity, because it was the mission at the core of its Lord's identity.

We Believe in One Baptism for the Forgiveness of Sins

Leanne Van Dyk

Theologians and pastors sometimes play an odd armchair sport—
"Find the Heresy." It may be less than a full game, appearing only as
a category on the game show *Jeopardy*. The category could be called
"Heresies Then and Now." In response to the "answer" *The assumption that all people are born good and innocent,* the player would press
the buzzer and "question," *What is Pelagianism?* The category might
continue with a more contemporary "answer," *The claim made by
advertisers that automobiles, cell phones, and tennis shoes can indeed fill
the deepest longing of the human heart.* The "question" would be, *What
is materialism?* The host might also accept *What is a phony, market-
driven eschatology?* Perhaps some of you have played the game. I know
I have.

CASUAL MODALISM

I like to play this game by observing the way church folk talk about
God. In adult education settings, for example, it is interesting to note
the questions that are asked and the assumptions that those questions
reveal. For example, one common assumption that emerges in

conversations with committed Christian believers is the "casual modalism" that Colin Gunton mentioned in his essay. It is convenient for people to think of God as present and active in the world alternately as Father, as Son, and as Holy Spirit.

Like many heresies, modalism has the benefit of being easily understood. Modalism presents a god who makes a divine decision on whether to be Father in any given case of divine action, or Son, or Spirit. The problem is that casual modalism, however convenient it may be conceptually, misses the full Trinitarian richness. Modalism's Trinitarian error is dividing the job descriptions of the triune God far too neatly. God the Father creates the world, upholds it, preserves it, and governs it. God the Son saves the world by dying for our sins and rising in victory. The job description of God the Holy Spirit is a little bit fuzzier, but it has something to do with giving spiritual gifts, illuminating the scriptures, warming our hearts, and inspiring our minds.

My description of casual modalism is not intended to caricature lay people. I do not mean to trivialize their theological and spiritual instincts, and I certainly don't intend to pin the label "heretic" on them so that I can smugly correct them. Quite the contrary; when I talk to lay people about the faith, I usually come away instructed, encouraged, and even corrected. What is true of adults is also true of children. In children, you can see theological reflection happening before your eyes. Recently I talked with two eight-year-old girls, working through some of the questions and answers of the new Presbyterian catechism, "Belonging to God." The catechism's first question is "Who are you?" The answer is "I am a child of God." The second question follows naturally: "What does it mean to be a child of God?" Answer: "That I belong to God, who loves me." The sequence continues: "What makes you a child of God?" with its answer, "Grace, God's free gift of love that do I not deserve and cannot earn." And then the obvious question: "Don't you have to be good for God to love you?" When I introduced that question for the first time, one of the girls said, "Yes, you do have to be good. God doesn't love you if you sin." The other girls looked at her in horror. "No, Kimberly, God loves us no matter what. God loves everybody." The answer in the catechism confirmed their deep theological instinct: God loves me in spite of all I do wrong. Thus have I learned to respect the theological wonderings of believers.

Yet, surely, one of the responsibilities of Christian pastors and theological educators is to identify and correct faulty understandings of God. This responsibility grows from the reality that some mistaken assumptions about God rob God of the full glory and honor due God. Moreover, they rob us of a full, rich, wondrously interesting understanding of God. The point is not to get the answers right on an exam. The point is to grow into the fullness of the grace of the Lord Jesus Christ, the love of God, and the communion of the Holy Spirit. Our knowledge of God is only partial, yet we have the responsibility to speak of God and of God's way among us using the complete palette of colors given to us in the scripture.

So, now, back to the common theological mistake that imagines God the Father creating, God the Son saving, and God the Spirit gifting. This three-way division of labor may be tidy, but it is not biblical. An unsurpassable passage in the first chapter of Colossians portrays the *full* range of divine activity and ascribes it to Jesus Christ:

> He is the image of the invisible God, the firstborn of all creation; for in him all things in heaven and on earth were created, things visible and invisible, whether thrones or dominions or rulers or powers—all things have been created through him and for him. He himself is before all things, and in him all things hold together. He is the head of the body, the church; he is the beginning, the firstborn from the dead, so that he might come to have first place in everything. For in him all the fullness of God was pleased to dwell, and through him God was pleased to reconcile to himself all things, whether on earth or in heaven, by making peace through the blood of his cross. (Col. 1:15–20)

Here Jesus Christ is the agent of creation, the sustainer of all things, the establisher of the church, and the goal of all history. Clearly, the truth about Jesus Christ is much bigger than the cross and the empty tomb, central and necessary as they are in the Christian faith.

Likewise, the work of the Holy Spirit in scripture is varied. Scripture ascribes to the Spirit a cosmic range of activity. The Spirit creates and maintains life. The Spirit apportions gifts. The Spirit reveals God in prophecy. The Spirit lifts up, heals, liberates. The opening verses of Isaiah 61 are one example of the splendid diversity of the Spirit's activity:

> The Spirit of the Lord GOD is upon me,
>   because the LORD has anointed me;
> he has sent me to bring good news to the oppressed,
>   to bind up the brokenhearted,
> to proclaim liberty to the captives,
>   and release to the prisoners;
> to proclaim the year of the LORD's favor,
>   and the day of vengeance of our God;
>   to comfort all who mourn.
>
> (Isaiah 61:1–2)

All this shalom-spreading, justice-building, peace-planting activity is because the *Spirit of the Lord* is upon the prophet. And, of course, these are the words that Jesus himself used in the synagogue to describe his own ministry.

The biblical picture of the activity of God, then, is not neatly divided up among Trinitarian persons. Although it is roughly correct to appropriate certain divine acts to the Father, other divine acts to the Son, and other divine acts to the Spirit, this must not become a rigid division of labor. If we divide and separate the gracious actions of our God, our understanding of God is limited, and so our worship of God is impaired and our service of God is hindered. We find ourselves actually restricting God, theologizing away God's expansive freedom, inventive grace, and boundary-erasing love.

SALVATION FROM THE PERSPECTIVE OF THE SPIRIT

This theological convocation [see the Introduction] is focused on the Spirit, the Lord, the giver of life. My own task is to remind us all of the wide-angle of the Spirit's work, the expansive terrain over which the Holy Spirit freely moves, the always creative, sometimes surprising, frequently inventive strategies of the Holy Spirit. More particularly, my task is to think of salvation from the perspective of the Holy Spirit. This is what the phrase "One baptism for the forgiveness of sins" refers to—an understanding of salvation from the perspective of the Spirit. Toward the end of his life, Karl Barth had "a beautiful dream," as he put it. He wondered about the possibility of a Christian theology that would be focused on the Holy Spirit, so that all of theology would be illuminated by the doctrine of the Holy Spirit. Christology would be understood in relationship to the Holy Spirit, as would justification and sanctification, creation, and eschatology. Rather than a Christocentric theology, Barth imagined a pneumacentric theology. It would be, of course foolish for me to pretend to fulfill Barth's beautiful dream here, but we may be able to join him in wondering about a Christian theology from the perspective of the Holy Spirit.

First, I would like to identify resources within the classic Reformed tradition for a Spirit-oriented perspective on salvation. Recall the way Calvin begins Book III of his *Institutes*. You will remember that Book II is about Jesus Christ, especially chapters 12–17. Here we encounter the material on the necessity of the incarnation, focusing on the Chalcedonian affirmation of Jesus Christ as fully divine and fully human. Here we also encounter the material on the threefold office of Jesus—prophet, priest, and king. And here we find the section on the atonement, how Christ accomplished our redemption. Calvin expounds the classic images of paying the price, winning the victory, and standing as our substitute. Thus we see in Book II a full and complete account of salvation, right? Not exactly.

The reader finishes Book II and turns the page to Book III. There he states, "We must now examine this question. How do we receive those benefits which the Father bestowed on his only-begotten Son?"[1] Calvin is asking how we get in on all this that Christ has done for us. He proceeds by declaring, "First, we must understand that as long as Christ remains outside of us, and we are separated from him, all that he has suffered and done for the salvation of the human race remains useless and of no value for us."[2] This is a very strong statement, indeed. I believe Calvin intends this dramatic assertion to create strong anxiety and tension in his readers. "All that he has suffered and done for the salvation of the human race remains useless and of no value for us," unless. . . . It is all good for nothing unless we are linked to the events that took place in the life, death, and resurrection of Jesus of Nazareth—unless we are connected, joined, and united to those events.

Calvin now shows us why he is sometimes called "the theologian of the Holy Spirit," for he resolves this acute tension by saying, "The

Holy Spirit is the bond by which Christ effectually unites us to himself."[3] It is by the Spirit that we are joined to Jesus Christ. It is by the Spirit that all that Jesus Christ has suffered and done for us is made actual, concrete, real. Furthermore, it is the Spirit that gifts us with the faith required to receive the faith of Christ. In a kind of wonderful Reformed circularity, the Spirit gives us faith that then, in turn, receives grace. Calvin's view of the work of the Spirit is exceedingly expansive. He says that the Spirit "not only quickens and nourishes us by a general power that is visible both in the human race and in the rest of the living creatures, but he is also the root and seed of heavenly life in us."[4]

If I am reading Calvin correctly, the Holy Spirit is the life principle of all created beings. It is the Spirit who liberally ushers in breath and pulse, muscle contraction and brain waves, sight and hearing of *all* living creatures, from gerbils to giraffes, from wombats to walruses to each of us here. The Spirit of God is your life principle, as Calvin puts it. If that isn't enough, the Spirit is also the source of heavenly life in us. It is the Spirit who allows us glimpses of God's presence in our own lives and in the lives of those we love. It is the Spirit who guarantees our place in the new heaven and the new earth, that final victory of God's shalom.

You may remember that in the rest of Book III, Calvin lays out the shape of the link between Christ and the believer, accomplished by the Spirit. His chapters on justification, sanctification, repentance, self-denial, Christian freedom, prayer, and even election are all topics that illustrate the basic principle that our salvation is made real, concrete, and vivid in the Spirit. We sometimes think of salvation as an "above us" reality, something done in a heavenly courtroom or in a cosmic battle between the armies of God and the armies of Satan. Once the verdict is reached or the battle is won, we are pronounced "saved." This is a familiar but reductionist understanding of salvation. Like all reductionism there is something to this that is right, of course, even profoundly right. Martin Luther's restlessness over his own inadequacies was put to rest only when he realized that he did not need to earn his own salvation, for God had justified him once and for all, freely, in Jesus Christ. The once-for-all-ness of salvation, the reality that salvation is not dependent on us, must always be a touchstone of Christian faith.

Even so, to think of salvation only as an "above us" reality—as something that happened back then, over there, up high—is to forget about the incarnation, the flesh and blood, life and death, of our Lord Jesus Christ. When Jesus proclaimed the kingdom of God, he interpreted it as release for the prisoners, recovery of sight for the blind, healing of the sick—all indicating a salvation that is immersed in earthly, physical, daily life. It is also to forget the Holy Spirit, for it is the Spirit who links the events of the cross and the empty tomb, and it is the Spirit who makes those events our events.

Lutheran theologian Helmut Thielicke issues a caution at this point. He wants to emphasize the givenness of the cross and the empty tomb. He does not question that these events must become actual and real and present in the life of the believer. But he draws our attention to the fact that the Spirit's role is not only to make those events our events, but also to refer us back again and again to the historical person and work of Christ. Throughout his three-volume work, *The Evangelical Faith,* Thielicke repeatedly makes the point that the salvation event—though the work of the Holy Spirit—is not only a present experience but also a real, past event.[5] Two foci are important then: past event and present salvation. Both are guaranteed by the Holy Spirit.

Our second move in exploring salvation from the perspective of the Holy Spirit is to listen to contemporary voices from the Reformed tradition. These voices begin with Calvin's basic insight that we are linked to salvation through the Holy Spirit, that past events become our events through the Spirit. This insight is then made concrete and particular by illustrating it, imagining it, and hoping it. In his book *God the Spirit,* Michael Welker never tires of reminding us that God's reality is much richer than the forms into which we attempt to make God fit.[6] He goes on to say that human reality is also much richer than the forms into which we attempt to make humans fit. He celebrates the differences, the multiforms, the particularities of human existence as a wonderful flourish of our creator God. Welker suggests that the Spirit works in the details, the particulars of human life.

The twelfth chapter of Paul's first letter to the Corinthians concerns the wide variety of spiritual gifts, making the crucial claim that the same Spirit gives all the different gifts. Paul couples this with the equally crucial claim that it is through these diverse gifts that the community is united into one body. The Spirit both differentiates and unites. As Welker puts it, "The unity of the Spirit becomes a reality, not by imposing an illusory homogeneity, but by cultivating creaturely difference and by removing unrighteous differences."[7] Now, if the Spirit works in the concrete, actual particulars of human life, it is clear that an incarnational Christian theology should not confess its faith in a vague, general, indefinite spirit. An incarnational Christian theology confesses its faith in the Holy Spirit, the Lord, the giver of life—specific, particular, concrete life. And if the Spirit is in the concrete, actual particulars of life, then salvation through Jesus Christ must become visible in the lived experiences of human beings and human communities.

This does not mean that salvation is created by human beings and human communities, of course. The Holy Spirit makes concrete and vivid in our lives all that Christ accomplished for us. But it does mean that salvation from the perspective of the Spirit is actual, concrete, visible, particular, and noticeable. One can see it. One can sense the quality of it. One can be drawn into it. All this is done by the Holy Spirit.

Let me elaborate on this compelling point. I tend to focus, even to obsess, on certain texts in scripture for weeks at a time. I am a theology professor, not a parish minister, and so I have the luxury of wallowing around in scripture rather than having to get down to business and write a sermon. As I wallow, I try to understand the layers of meaning in a text. I try to discern what I'm missing, and what fresh gift there might be. Lately my focus has been on the fruit of the Spirit passage in Galatians 5. Like many of you, I grew up in a Christian home. I learned each fruit of the Spirit by memorizing them and even singing songs about them. As a child, I understood these fruits to be a short list of requirements for Christian behavior. I assumed that the fruits were a checklist against which I was to note my own behavior, which frequently fell far short. I was not always a patient, longsuffering, and self-controlled child. Only recently (I am a slow learner) have I realized that the text is not a checklist, but a concrete, vivid picture of what it looks like when the gospel becomes embodied in a human person. If we wonder what salvation looks like, what face it has, how it is clothed, this is it: love, joy, peace, patience, kindness, generosity, faithfulness, gentleness, and self-control. If we understand salvation to be the actual, lived reality of the Spirit linking us to Jesus Christ, and we want to know what it looks like when past events become our events, here it is! Salvation is a present reality by the power of the Holy Spirit.

A colleague of mine at Western Seminary, Jim Brownson, puts it this way, "To speak of salvation without also speaking of repentance, the freedom of the Spirit, the forgiveness of sins, participation in the redeemed community, and the transformation toward a new and holy life, is to speak of a meaningless salvation, abstract and devoid of content. To claim that salvation is present where these realities are not experienced is to strip salvation of most of its content for Christians. One wonders whether Christians' discussions of salvation become so otherworldly at times because we lose a firm grip on what it means to be a redeemed community in the here and now."

BAPTIZED

Finally, we come to baptism. Although the phrase of the Creed I am considering here is "one baptism for the forgiveness of sins," I have not yet mentioned baptism because we first needed to look at salvation from the perspective of the Holy Spirit. Before considering baptism, we thought about the Spirit linking us to Jesus Christ, we explored how salvation must be lived, experienced, and actualized, and we affirmed that past events must become our concretely visible events.

Now we can claim that baptism is the dramatic, visible model of salvation understood from the perspective of the Spirit. Baptism is the sacrament uniquely suited to be a window on the reality of salvation. Why? Because baptism is the sacramental act that unites us to all the realities of salvation that the Holy Spirit confers on us and makes concretely visible in our lived experience. Baptism, through the power of the Holy Spirit, unites us to the reality of the forgiveness of sins, union with Christ, incorporation into the community, dying and rising with Christ. Baptism dramatically and visibly acts out salvation through the perspective of the Holy Spirit. We can examine only a few of baptism's multivalent realities.

First, baptism is the drama of our incorporation into the community. The best way to tell this is to borrow a story from Presbyterian pastor Michael Lindvall. In *Good News from North Haven*, Lindvall's narrator tells the story of little Jimmy's baptism. Jimmy's mother, Tina, was a young unwed mother who had requested baptism for her infant son. The elders of the church were concerned, anxious not to be seen as endorsing lax moral standards. Yet, they consented. On the morning of the baptism, Tina stood at the font with her baby. It was the long-standing custom of this congregation for close family members to stand as well, in promise and support for the child. Knowing that this baby had no such extended family, the minister of the congregation began to read the baptismal form.

> I was just about to ask Tina the parents' questions of commitment when I became aware of movement in the pews. Angus McDowell had stood up, Minnie beside him. Then a couple of elders stood up, then the sixth grade Sunday School teacher stood up; then a new young couple in the church and soon, before my incredulous eyes, the whole church was standing up with Jimmy. Tina was crying, of course, and Mildred Corey was holding onto the pew in front of her as though she was standing on the deck of a ship rolling in a great wind, which, in a way, she was.[8]

That story makes concrete and particular what incorporation into the community of Christ means. Being united in Christ, in the community, is not all that baptism means, of course. Baptism is not only standing in solidarity with a single mother in difficult circumstances, but it is *at least* that. It seems to me that there are two parallel tracks in the journey of growing into a faith that is mature and seasoned and wise. One track is an expanding awareness of all that is mysterious and unknowable about God. Many of the contemplatives and mystics of the Christian tradition knew that. The other track is the sort of stubborn insistence that there must be seeable, knowable, visible signs of authentic Christian living. Both tracks are laid down by the Holy Spirit.

Second, baptism is the drama of our new identity in Jesus Christ. Baptism, through the power of the Holy Spirit, confers on us a new reality and inaugurates us into a new era. Excitement about the new millennium is nothing compared to the new era signified by baptism. But it is strangely easy for us to forget our identity in Jesus Christ, to neglect the reality of dying and rising with Christ and being raised to new life in Christ. We suffer from chronic amnesia about the most fundamental reality of our lives—that we belong to Jesus Christ in life and in death.

There are an increasing number of nursing facilities dedicated to the care and well-being of persons with Alzheimer's disease. Some of the professionals on these units are called MLAs—Memory Loss Assistants. MLAs talk to the patients and read them books. They work through series of patterning exercises and assist patients to retain various basic life functions for as long as possible. When they talk to Alzheimer's patients, they remind them of their names. They remind them of the names of their family members and friends, and they show pictures of family events. The MLAs rehearse this over and over again—who the patients are, who their family is, what the significant events of their past are. Baptism is a sacramental Memory Loss Assistant. We are all Alzheimer's patients in the Christian faith. Daily we need to be reminded who we are, what our names are, who our family is, who we belong to. Baptism links us to these most fundamental realities.

Third, baptism is the drama of the reality of the forgiveness of sins. One baptism for the forgiveness of sins, the Creed says. Clearly, this particular promise of the sacrament of baptism has been important enough to the long witness of the church to give it precious space in the Creed. We do not need to rehearse old arguments about baptismal regeneration, or tired debates about believer baptism versus infant baptism. Surely, baptismal water does not effect the forgiveness of our sins. Paul said, "In Christ God was reconciling the world to himself" (2 Cor. 5:19). But, just as surely, baptismal water is the effective means of grace that God intends and promises. The water of baptism joins our life to Christ forevermore. The one baptism for the forgiveness of sins has actual, present, concrete reality. It is not general, vague, or abstract. It is as present as today . . . as close as our neighbor, spouse, or friend . . . as real as the glimmerings of justice, mercy, and hope that we see in the world. Yes, the world is sad and broken. It is painfully divided by race, religion, and ethnicity. But, thanks be to God, there are divine sparks, eschatological outbreaks of justice and shalom in the world, and all of this is the concrete reality of the forgiveness of sins. Wolfhart Pannenberg makes this clear throughout his

Systematic Theology whenever he stresses the fact that salvation given in Jesus Christ is not only a future event but also a present experience.[9]

I have repeatedly emphasized that the Holy Spirit's action in salvation is making the gospel's past events our events. Thielicke improves on this when he says that the Holy Spirit makes present the past event of salvation and also the future of salvation. What is required of us as we look at salvation from the perspective of the Spirit is both a more microscopic view and a more telescopic view. Our understanding of salvation must include the particular, the vivid, the concrete, the actual present reality of salvation. It must also include the cosmic, the eschatological, the yearning for the restoration of full shalom in the new heaven and the new earth.

NOTES

1. John Calvin, *Institutes of the Christian Religion,* Library of Christian Classics, ed. John T. McNeill, trans. Ford Lewis Battles (Philadelphia: Westminster Press, 1960), 3.1.1.
2. Ibid.
3. Ibid.
4. Ibid., 3.1.2.
5. Helmut Thielicke, *The Evangelical Faith,* 3 vols. (Macon, Ga.: Smyth and Helwys, 1997).
6. Michael Welker, *God the Spirit,* trans. John F. Hoffmeyer (Minneapolis: Fortress Press, 1994).
7. Ibid., p. 25.
8. Lindvall, Michael L., *The Good News from North Haven: A Year in the Life of a Small Town* (New York: Doubleday, 1991), p. 174.
9. Wolfhart Pannenberg, *Systematic Theology* (Grand Rapids, Mich.: Eerdmans, 1991).

CONTEMPORARY ISSUES

Why the Holy Spirit Now?

The Promise and Peril of Recent Interest in the Holy Spirit

Gregory Anderson Love

In his recent book *The God We Never Knew,* New Testament scholar Marcus Borg says he grew up as a Lutheran in North Dakota imagining God "as a supernatural being 'out there,' separate from the world, who created the world a long time ago and who may from time to time intervene within it."[1] Borg continues, "In an important sense, this God is not 'here' and thus cannot be known or experienced but only believed in."[2] Borg eventually found such a God—the familiar "old man in the sky"— incredible and irrelevant, and he believes many Christians today have also. Instead of this conception, he proposes an alternate vision of God— not the *supernatural being* "out there," but rather the *encompassing Spirit,* a nonmaterial dimension of reality all around us. "God is more than the universe," says Borg, "yet we and the universe are 'in God.' Thus, in a spatial sense, God is not 'somewhere else' but 'right here.'[3] Borg calls this concept of God *panentheism,* meaning "everything existing in God." Quoting Bonhoeffer, Borg states that "God is the beyond in our midst."[4]

In his 1997 book on the Holy Spirit, *The Source of Life,* Jürgen Moltmann seems to say similar things:

> The world is full of praise, for God is in this world. God
> is not far off, in the Beyond, but is himself the life in the

> world. Israel expressed this by saying that God's Spirit,
> God's Wisdom and God's presence fill everything cre-
> ated in such a way that all things live from God and have
> their existence and continuance in God.[5]

Like Borg, Moltmann rejects an image of God as the lonely Monarch in the sky, ruling over all things from a distance, and instead proposes his own form of panentheism, "everything existing in God," based on the interactive presence of the triune God in this world.

In the similarities between Borg's and Moltmann's panentheistic reconceptions of God's relation to the world, we find the great promise of recent interest in the Holy Spirit. In the differences between their types of panentheism, the great danger of such interest is revealed. All language about God the Spirit is not the same.

I will begin by describing briefly the strengths of recent discussions of the Spirit. I will quickly move into a discussion of the dangers, however, by contrasting Borg's understanding of the Spirit with Moltmann's. While the language seems similar, their panentheistic concepts of God are radically different. This comparison will show the weaknesses of those current discussions of the Spirit that are not well funded by the tradition's understanding of the Trinity. I will conclude by returning to the positive, showing how Moltmann's panentheistic view of God the Spirit contributes to a dynamic understanding of prayer.

STRENGTHS OF RECENT INTEREST IN THE SPIRIT

If our Greek philosophical heritage pushed the West toward seeing relations between things in dualistic and hierarchical fashions, it is the Judeo-Christian doctrine of God the Spirit that allows us to see relations between things in holistic ways. As the "bond of love" between the Father and the Son (Augustine), the Spirit is able to connect things that are different without overcoming their uniqueness. This "matchmaking" role of the Spirit is evident in five strengths of recent discussions of the Spirit.

First, recent discussions of the Spirit help to explain *how it is possible for God's will and activity and our human will and activity to come together* in a way that allows room for human freedom, imagination, and particularity, while also preserving the sovereign freedom and creativity of the Holy Spirit.

I will show later how the Spirit creates room for the coming together of God's will and our own in prayer, but I now want to show how the Spirit's role of conjoining two free wills can be seen in relation to Jesus. How is it possible for the divine nature and human nature to coexist so seamlessly in Jesus that he always acts as one person? How, for example, is the human Jesus able to resist temptation during his forty days in the wilderness (Luke 4)? As Colin Gunton points out, it is not primarily because Jesus is the Son of God incarnate. Rather, in the self-emptying, kenotic movement of the incarnation (Phil. 2:5–11), the second Person of the Trinity lays aside privileged attributes of deity. Without omniscience and omnipotence, the human Jesus is able to resist the temptation of evil, to remain human, to remain himself, binding his will to the will of God the Father. Jesus is able to do this because at every moment in the wilderness he relies on the power and comfort and guidance of the Holy Spirit, who helps Jesus to keep trusting God when things look grim.[6]

This renewed pneumatological emphasis impacts Christology by showing how it is possible for Jesus to be human, particular, and cre-ative while also having his will continuously unified with the will of God the Father. It allows for a *historical* Jesus that coheres with Jesus as incarnate second Person of the Trinity. As human, Jesus' messianic consciousness was not fully developed at birth, but grew along with his mind and personality. He had human temptations, fears, anxieties, and loneliness. As human, his ability to do miracles was based in power given to him by the accompanying Spirit. This self-emptying, incarnate second Person of the Trinity who is Spirit-led is *human,* like us, yet with his human mind and will always following the lead of his divine nature, which is determined to trust the Father. The Spirit, for Jesus and for us, acts as an *empowering presence* that enables us to be human.

A theological rule for language about the God-world relation is found within this pneumatologically balanced Christology. The immanent presence of the *transcendent* Spirit goes hand in hand with the increase of a "free space" between God and the world in which nat-ural processes and human agents may "be themselves." The sovereign presence and activity of the Spirit and the autonomy of the creature exist in a relation of direct, rather than inverse, proportion.

This rule of theological grammar goes against the modern Western assumption that the world is devoid of Spirit. Modern science, for example, has often seen the world's processes as ruled by supposedly "closed" naturalistic and materialistic forces of cause and effect that allow no place for divine involvement. This scientific reductionism strips our everyday lives of sacred moments. Combining such deism with Bultmann's view that God interacts only with the human soul, we humans could imagine having a vertical relation with God. But in our horizontal relations, the creature-to-creature relations that affect us deeply and with which we must grapple, God is absent. Our everyday experiences are devoid of the Spirit.

In contrast to naturalistic materialism, recent work on the Spirit allows us to recover a truth that Calvin always knew: *God the Spirit is present and active* in this world, whether we perceive the Spirit or not. Divine transcendence and divine immanence are correlative, not opposing, principles. Just as the incarnate Son of God is surrounded at all times by the guiding and comforting Spirit, so all creaturely existence is surrounded by the Spirit. God's Spirit is present in the deepest places: in the movements of the heart; in the spark of connection between two people; in the fecund glory of nature. Further, pneumatology confirms what people in Alcoholics Anonymous have long known: the Spirit is present with power that enables human transformation.

The modern mind often presents the believer with false options: Jesus is either divine or human; God is either transcendent, and thus not involved in its everyday life, or immanent, and thus indistinguishable from the world's existence. Recent work in pneumatology has shown how the placing of these pairs in relations of opposition is false. Similarly, the demand that the church use either male or female language for God presents a false choice. The presence of God the Spirit underneath all things, supporting new life and creaturely development, has rightly encouraged the church *to imagine the Spirit using female as well as male and impersonal metaphors.* For example, Elizabeth Johnson uses Hosea 13:8 to describe God as a "strong mother bear" who both nurtures and fights for the justice needed by her cubs.[7] God includes traits of both genders, yet transcends gender; thus it is appropriate to use female as well as male analogies for God. Furthermore, if God the Spirit is like this, then surely women created in God's image have a strong role of public agency.

The idea that God is interested either in human salvation or in the redemption of the whole created order presents another false choice. Recent pneumatology *moves us beyond exclusive human-centeredness to perceive God's care for the nonhuman creatures.* Moltmann recalls an ancient Syrian Christian name for the Spirit as "the mother of all life," just as she is "the mother of believers" in John 3.[8] God the Spirit's immanence shows God's particular care for all God's creatures; the Spirit who continuously gives life to all things also seeks their transformation into new wholeness.

Finally, pneumatology gives support to the idea that *God desires communities based in reciprocity and equality.* As Gunton says, the Holy Spirit is the creator of communities of conviviality and free interdependence, wherever they are to be found.[9] If all Christians receive the same Spirit at baptism, and all are brought into the same body of Christ, then to heed the Spirit's promptings is to encourage our unique gifts while depending mutually on one another.

BORG'S AND MOLTMANN'S PANENTHEISM

Recent discussions of the Spirit seek to overcome dualistic and hierarchical thinking, replacing them with with holistic views of the connections between all things: body and soul, humans and cosmos, God and the world. Panentheism, the view that God is present in the world and that the world exists in God, attempts the same thing. But it is precisely this Spirit-inspired panentheism that represents the danger as well as the promise of recent talk of the Spirit. Not all forms of panentheism are the same, however, and a comparison of Moltmann's and Borg's forms will reveal both the promise and the danger.

In *The Source of Life,* Jürgen Moltmann says that the Spirit of God, who is above us, in us, and round about us, encounters us as the great promise, the promise of a future healing which breaks into our world even now.[10] This theological statement embraces a complex form of panentheism, one that combines two different but compatible understandings of the Spirit's presence.

One one hand, Moltmann says that "God's Holy Spirit is experienced elementally, not personally."[11] He then uses two impersonal metaphors to describe how we exist "in God." First, in the Spirit we experience God as a *primal and all-embracing presence,* a "free space" in which we have time and room to grow.[12] Following Michael Welker,[13] Moltmann imagines the Holy Spirit as akin to a vibrating and vitalizing energy field.

When we are are surrounded by the beat of music and the rhythmic movement of people dancing, we too begin to tap our toes and get up and move. The music and movement create webs that connect us to others while allowing us space to be ourselves. In similar fashion, the Holy Spirit creates webs of connections between creatures, through which life is communicated and freedom encouraged. In that sense, the Spirit is immanent, around us and in us at every moment, and like a fetus in its mother's womb we live within these Spirit-created connections.

Along with the Spirit as matrix of connections and as space, we also experience the Spirit impersonally as *power.* The Holy Spirit acts as the "energy" of the Godhead, releasing the energies of the world.[14] We experience life as we are connected to the Spirit who pours life into us. The gifts of the Spirit, including the charismata, come from the *charis* and energies that emanate from the Spirit.

While the Spirit is appropriately described impersonally, however, as the divinely created "space" in which we are free to dance, and as the "fountain of life" (Ps. 36:9), such descriptions of God's immanent presence are insufficient. The Spirit is a life force, but also more than that. The Spirit is the presence of God in person, as *a divine counterpart, a personal "Other."*[15] This divine counterpart, who provides a nurturing presence all around us, approaches us within that "free space" to speak and listen. God the Spirit is an *engaging* presence, a sovereign partner who accompanies us, challenging our self-deceptions and calling us into the new humanity of God's inbreaking future.

The criterion for "testing the spirits" is whether the Spirit is tied inextricably to the face of Christ. Does the Spirit enable people to call on Jesus with the sign of the cross as the source of hope? Or do those who experience a "spiritual presence" end up ecstatically calling on some other power for aid? There can be no Pentecost presence of the Spirit without Good Friday and Easter.

This is where Borg's alternative form of panentheism falters. Like

Moltmann, Borg uses impersonal metaphors of *space* and *power* to describe the Spirit's immanent presence. For Borg, God encompasses and permeates all things, and all things exist *in God*. But Borg is unclear about the sense in which he means the preposition "in." As he explains God's transcendence in the first three chapters of *The God We Never Knew,* Borg says three times that God is "other than" the universe (pp. 26, 32, 46). But seven times he says that God is transcendent because God is "more than" the universe (pp. 26, 27, 32, 33, 46, 72, 76). This latter phrase, precisely because it is vague, could easily suggest that God is in the world and the world is "in God" because God and the world share the same being, the same substance: God simply has more of it. The world would be seen as God's body, an emanation of God's being.

What is lost in Borg's discussion of God as Spirit is *the qualitative distinction between God and the world,* between Creator and creature. What is lost, further, is the complex idea that while God is indeed *the womb and free space in which we grow,* the Spirit is also *the angry mother bear who demands justice* for all her offspring. When the Israelites worshiped the Canaanite fertility gods, they forgot the same thing, so God raised up the prophets and poured the Spirit on them. The Spirit engaged the Israelites personally, with judgment and a call to change.

Moltmann avoids the dangers into which Borg falls. While Moltmann describes the Spirit as the "well of life" and the "broad space" in which we live, he never says that God is "more than" the world. The God who created all things through the Word by the power of the Spirit is not the world, but rather the world's source and sustenance and end. Moltmann goes on to say that impersonal metaphors for the Spirit must be countered with personal ones, and the Person of the Spirit must be tied to the Person of Christ and to Christ's messianic mission.

Ultimately, Borg reveals the danger of recent talk of the Spirit. If discussion of the Spirit focuses primarily on impersonal metaphors for the Spirit's presence and power, and if the understanding of the Spirit's character is funded mainly by a creation theology and present experiences of the Spirit, rather than by the Spirit's role in the narrative of redemption witnessed to in scripture, then it is likely that the qualitative distinction between the Holy Spirit and earthly spirits will be blurred or lost altogether. When this happens, it will also be forgotten that the Spirit who brings life also brings the promise and demands of new life to a sinful humanity. We need a complex form of panentheism. We must remember that the Spirit, who as our mother creates a safe space in which to grow, also points to the One who says, "Come, follow me."

PRAYER AND THE TWOFOLD WORK OF THE TRANSCENDENT SPIRIT

If we are fortunate as children, Moltmann says, we experience our primary caregiver as a personal presence surrounding us, creating a space in which we are free to learn and develop at our own pace, and as a personal counterpart who engages us verbally and nonverbally.[16] In this human experience of a caring father or mother, Moltmann sees an analogy to the Spirit's presence—elementally as *presence* and *empowering power,* and personally as *counterpart.* He also sees them together in the image of creation as a "house" in which God and creature live beside each other eschatologically, sharing space and interacting with each other.[17] If the world is a "house," both it and its relations are creaturely, not divine; and yet God is not absent from the house, but present within it to create its life and soul. To say that we "live and move and have our being in God" is to say that we live in the creaturely house in which God dwells beside us. It certainly does not mean that our being somehow shares in divine being.

This image of God the Spirit as dwelling within the house called our heart, providing both *elemental space* and *personal engagement,* is used by Ann and Barry Ulanov to explain the relation between divine and human activity in prayer. In their book *Primary Speech,* the Ulanovs claim that the fall of humanity manifests itself in the splitting of the self. Buried beneath the "pretended self" that we project to others lies our "primary self." In Augustinian fashion, the primary self is driven by two basic emotions, fear and desire, and by "a wrenching need for wholeness" found in the life of community.[18] Yet out of fear that our needs will not be met, we hide and suppress our moral guilt, our longings, our anger. We grasp for finite things to fill our longings for the infinite.

In prayer, however, the object of our prayer—God—leads to "an enlargement of the self."[19] In prayer, two divine forces are involved: "The God who came to us in the flesh," and "the Spirit who dwells in our flesh."[20] The Ulanovs then describe two works of the Spirit in relation to our human imagination. First, the Spirit *spurs our imagination toward fantasy.* Through bringing our fantasies to consciousness in prayer, the Spirit *creates a free space* in which we can speak what it is we are feeling beneath our "pretended selves." When we look consciously at our fantasies, they become a window to what is really going on with us, showing us the internal fears and desires that motivate our behavior. Initially, the Spirit's encouraging of our fantasies may feed our primary emotions and experiences, including our sinful ones of hatred, greed and envy, despair and distraction, addiction, and self-hatred. By bringing these primary emotions to the surface, the Spirit shows "our own perjury against truth."[21]

The second work of the Spirit is what the Ulanovs call "the purgation of prayer" and "the process of dis-identification."[22] The Spirit dialogues with our human spirit to show us that what we imagine to be true about ourselves and our needs is not who we really are. Further, the Spirit shows us that our identity is reflected and found in Christ's humanity. Through the rhythmic movement and alterations in the acceptance of our fantasies and in bringing them to God the Father through the Son in the power of the Spirit, our images both of God and of self are "stripped" and cleansed. We are enabled by the Spirit and the Word to identify our true fears, longings, and need for God, and to claim them as our own.

The Ulanovs show how the immanent presence of the transcendent Spirit moves our human spirit into its own true freedom, both by creating a space for free imagination around us, and by engaging us within that space through dialogue. In similar fashion, Moltmann is able to understand the Spirit as surrounding our daily lives, yet in a way that is qualitatively different from the Spirit's presence with other creatures. He does this by including impersonal images for the Spirit's presence of space and power within the more primary personal image for the Spirit of divine counterpart. This imagines God in the world, and the world in God, in a way that conforms to the Bible's narrative of the triune God who loves this world passionately.

NOTES

1. Marcus J. Borg, *The God We Never Knew* (San Francisco: Harper-SanFrancisco, 1997), p. 11.
2. Ibid., pp. 11–12.
3. Ibid.
4. Ibid., p. 32.
5. Jürgen Moltmann, *The Source of Life: The Holy Spirit and the Theology of Life* (Minneapolis: Fortress Press, 1997), p. 133.
6. See Colin Gunton, *The Promise of Trinitarian Theology* (Edinburgh: T. & T. Clark, 1991), pp. 37, 67–70, 100, 134–36.
7. Elizabeth A. Johnson, *She Who Is: The Mystery of God in Feminist Theological Discourse* (New York: Crossroad, 1992), p. 180.
8. Moltmann, *Source of Life*, pp. 35, 114.
9. See Gunton, *Promise,* pp. 12, 50, 65, 76, 86, 91, 125, 133, 136.
10. Moltmann, *Source of Life*, p. 39.
11. Ibid., p. 69.
12. For the conception of the Spirit as the creator of "personal space" in which the creature has room to grow, see also Gunton, *Promise,* pp. 111–13, 131–33, 136–38.
13. Michael Welker, *God the Spirit* (Minneapolis: Fortress, 1994).
14. See Gunton, *Promise,* p. 158.
15. As Gunton also says, the Holy Spirit is "not some immanent and impersonal causal force but a free and personal other" (*Promise,* 134).
16. Moltmann, *Source of Life*, p. 11.
17. Ibid., p. 117.
18. Ann and Barry Ulanov, *Primary Speech* (Atlanta: John Knox Press, 1982), pp. 18–19.
19. Ibid., p. 17.
20. Ibid., p. 7.
21. Ibid., pp. 38–39.
22. Ibid., pp 42–43.

Holy Spirit and Human Spirit
Overcoming a Deceived Heart

Willie James Jennings

What does it mean to be self-deceived? What does it mean to have one's life trapped in self-deception? How is self-deception overcome? These are basic questions of the Christian life, basic questions that are also at the heart of pastoral ministry. I want to suggest to you that answering these basic questions allows us in a very important way to consider afresh the relation of the Holy Spirit to the human spirit. I want to suggest that the overcoming of self-deception is exactly the *appearing* of the relation between the Holy Spirit and the human spirit.

There is a deep connection between these basic pastoral questions and the Holy Spirit's relation to us, a deep connection that needs to be surfaced in our time. The reasons why we need its reemergence are complex, but the primary reason has to do with the growing confusion concerning the nature and contour of the inner life. On the one hand, the consideration of self-deception—whether broached in discussions of moral formation, pastoral care, or systematic theology—often lacks signs of having been born out of a deep theological vision. On the other hand, most discussions of spiritual presence and spiritual awareness in texts on theology or spirituality tend to create more questions about the identity of the Spirit (and God) than they address.

But such discussions also betray a deep bias toward a vision of the inner life that is consumed by self-interpretation and is subtly yet doggedly antinomian.

I would like to recapture a notion of self-deception that works in the service of pneumatology. I want to interweave the ways we might speak about both self-deception and the relation of the Holy Spirit to the human spirit. But I do this with a view toward modernity's effects on Western ideas about the inner life. I will begin with an important illustration of a modernity effect by looking briefly at Freud's famous essay on religion, *The Future of an Illusion.*[1] Then I will turn our attention to resources helpful for this recapturing: first, a section from Karl Barth's *Church Dogmatics* in which Barth discusses the relation of the soul to the body,[2] and second, aspects of Augustine's vision of the inner life as it is displayed in his text *The Spirit and the Letter.*[3] Together these authors will help us locate a theologically sensitive vision of self-deception.

FREUD'S ILLUSION: OUR DECEPTION

Freud wrote his now-famous text *The Future of an Illusion* in 1927 (*Die Zukunft einer Illusion,* first translated into English in 1928). It established him as what Ricoeur famously termed a "master of suspicion."[4] This text did not inaugurate Freud's critique of religion, for among this genre of writings are Freud's other famed texts, *Totem and Taboo* (1913), *Civilization and Its Discontents* (1930), and *Moses and Monotheism* (1939), all of which have their place in the canon of psychoanalytical literature. Yet *The Future of an Illusion* remains a masterpiece, because it gives witness to Freud's extraordinarily captivating imagination. Freud imagined a way of capturing the truth about the world and ourselves that opened possibilities for reinterpreting both at the same time. Freud made interpretation of our world and of the self one inseparable and continuous act.

Freud's goal is to show what is at stake for the future of societies in light of the existence of religious beliefs and practices. Religion comes into view as an absolutely crucial indicator of a society's past, present, and future. Freud's goal is not simply to expose the nature of the consciousness or unconsciousness of the individual, but to expose the collective, the political, unconscious.⁵ Freud's central point is clear and haunting: religious beliefs and practices are about desire. *Because* they are about desire, they are illusions. "Thus we call a belief an illusion," says Freud, "when a wish-fulfillment is a prominent factor in its motivation, and in doing so we *disregard* its relations to reality, just as the illusion itself sets no store by verification."⁶

Freud retreats from a straightforward fight with particular religious beliefs or practices concerning their truth or their correspondence to reality. His assault on them is much subtler, in that he posits a constellation of needs that interpenetrate religious belief and practice. Michael Palmer aptly delineates these needs as (1) the need to "come to terms with the external forces of nature which threaten to destroy humanity," (2) the need to "come to terms with the internal forces of nature, that is, human instincts which are no less threatening," and (3) the need to "satisfy our universal longing for the father-figure."⁷ Freud's mapping of desire on top of religious belief and practice is powerful and opens the door to a rhetorical question that, once asked, it seems impossible for us to redirect, thwart, or resist submission to its vast implications.

Freud asked implicitly and explicitly, Why do we adhere to ancient beliefs and practices, the beliefs and practices of our ancestors? His answer? We want what our ancestors wanted—ways of coping with our sense of helplessness in the world. The difference between our religious ancestors and us is that we have advanced. Our advance does not lie in the development of more sophisticated ways of coping with nature, but in our capacity to lay conscious claim on our collective self-deception, a self-deception we share with our ancestors. We desire (probably more sharply that those before us) a world free of violence, destruction, and chaos—a world in which we are not controlled by fear. Religious belief and practice have wonderfully, though not unambiguously, promoted such a world.

The ambiguity of religious belief and practice in promoting civilization, that is, in establishing society, is the switch Freud turns on to cast light on us. Freud contends that we should no longer adhere to religious beliefs and practices, not because they are false or wrong, but because they are imprecise.

Freud held that people believe out of self-deception. That is, our beliefs (our doctrines and practices) come into being as we navigate

the primordial sources of desire, the things that make for the formation of desire. Beliefs, formed by desire, promote an ethic for peace-
ful, safe, and structured society. However the navigation itself is
hidden from us, hidden by us, this inner truth guides the ship through
and around those primordial sources. We must understand this calculus of desire in order to bring to the surface of the self, to bring to
conscious awareness, the effects our world has on the formation of our
desire. More importantly, only by penetrating into the calculus of
desire can we clarify the moral and ethical practices that should continue to compel us.

Desire is concealed beneath the surface of the self and the actions
of any particular people or culture. This point is central to Freud's treatment of religion. Between thought (and the articulation of thought)
and awareness of the self is desire and its world of constitutive elements. What are our shared needs born of desire? Self-deception is the
refusal to consider these needs. There is a transparency of the self that
may be achieved by the proper interrogation of religious belief and
practice. In an extraordinary section of *The Future of an Illusion,* Freud
creates a conversation with a protagonist who accepts Freud's vision of
religion as self-deception, but turns that vision on its head. The protagonist tells Freud that all social doctrine, whether born of religion or
science, is illusion. The protagonist begins her challenge:

> That sounds splendid! A race of men who have
> renounced all illusions and have thus become capable of
> making their existence on earth tolerable. I, however,
> cannot share your expectations. . . . If you want to expel
> religion from our European civilization, you can only do
> it by means of another system of doctrines; and such a
> system would from the outset take over all the psycho-
> logical characteristics of religion—the same sanctity,
> rigidity, and intolerance, the same prohibition of
> thought—for its own defense. . . . Your endeavors come
> down to an attempt to replace a proved and emotionally
> valuable illusion by another one, which is unproved and
> without emotional value.[8]

In her point concerning the emotional value of religious belief and
practice, Freud's rhetorical protagonist gives us a strategy for showing
religion's continuing worth. The protagonist tells us that doctrines

and religious practices open the door into the inner life of the self or a society. Religion brings into view a powerful bulwark against the chaos of violence and destruction. Religion illuminates the ways in which the self and society remain stable in the face of senseless suffering. Thus religion constitutes the necessary first step in the moral development of a person or a people. The protagonist suggests that this first step may lead to "a refinement and sublimation of ideas, which make it possible for it [that is, the self and society] to be divested of most of the traces which it bears of primitive or infantile thinking."[9]

In this protagonist, Freud creates an enlightened religious advocate. In her view, faith and doctrine are useful in creating the first step in overcoming self-deception. Yet Freud, in the end, destroys the opponent he has created. He agrees with her regarding the value of religion and the illusionary nature of any social doctrine based on the "primacy of the intellect" (p. 66). But Freud contends that his own illusions are not, like the religious ones, incapable of correction. They do not have the character of a delusion, that is, an idea held in spite of its demonstrable falsehood. Freud states, "If experience should show not to me but to others after me who think as I do, that we have been mistaken, we will give up our expectations." Freud goes on to point out that while all knowledge of the self is contingent, once we have some knowledge of how the self works we must build from there, not pretending that aspects of the inner life have not been exposed.[10]

The specifics of many of Freud's theories have been abandoned, and his fundamental inventions of the consciousness have been discredited.[11] Freud remains important, however, because a Freudian architecture still informs much of our self-interpretation. For Freud, self-deception can be seen in the interplay of agency and structure, of the volitional and structuring forces of the self. In this regard, few have questioned the connection between desire and doctrinal formulation. Freud convinced us that beliefs are deeply connected to a matrix of multiple reckonings with our helplessness in the face of nature and the social world's chaotic power, with our negotiation with instinctual drives, and with the formational power of our parents on us (though not necessarily in that order).

More significantly, the Freudian affect still reaches far into our vision of social space. For Freud we must look, as through a transparency, at the practices and doctrines of a people—especially a religious people—in order to grasp the desires that give life and definition to those doctrines and practices.[12] Only by looking through beliefs to desires may we grasp the authentic sources of doctrinal adherence. The point for us is that, since Freud, overcoming self-deception requires that we enter into a deep self-interrogation that includes an interrogation of our relationships, our social space, and our society. This interrogation begins with the continuous questioning of why we adhere to religious belief and practice.

Rowan Williams suggests that with Freud we acquire an obsession with interiority (an inner life) that holds an imprisoned self.[13] Equally consequential, however, we receive from Freud a vision of self-deception that resists a theological understanding of the self. With Freud we acquire a vision of the self that defines religious doctrine and practice as nothing more than signifiers of the machinations of desire. Religious beliefs tells us who we are insofar as they reveal the unfolding drama of our psyche as it responds to the specifics of its existence.

Let us pose some questions to Freud, however. What if doctrine, specifically Christian doctrine and practice, establishes a vision of the self without the need for a transparent self? Moreover, what if Christian faith shows no imprisoned self, no inner child birthed by desire's working beneath the surface of the body, but rather the Spirit of God working in us by love? This would mean that what is in us is always "outside of us," before us, yet always at work on us. Let us begin to consider these questions with Barth's treatment of soul and body.

BARTH'S BODY AND SOUL: A NEW INNER LIFE

Barth turns us toward the second part of the problem we must face in order to recapture an understanding of self-deception that is deeply informed by pneumatology. The problem is simply that the idea of a human spirit has been characterized by modernity's vision of the imprisoned self. Even without Freud, talk of the human spirit evokes a vision of a transparent self that is connected to the divine at a sub-doctrinal level, at a level beneath adherence to any particular set of religious practices. The Enlightenment introduced important shifts in the way Christians spoke about the human spirit. Thus, *formal* discussion of the human spirit's relation to the Holy Spirit represents a fairly new kind of theological discourse. This, in turn, is in tension with ancient Christian ways of speaking about the relation of the Holy Spirit to human creatures. This tension exposes alternative ways of viewing the spiritual self.[14]

Mark McIntosh puts it well when he states that our modern constructs of the spiritual life have before them one of two options. The spiritual life may be understood either in terms of "a relationship between the creator and the creature . . . enacted in irreducibly historical terms," or "an inherent aspect of human subjectivity that is everywhere always the same." Either we have "the gospel sense of the slow and costly strain of discipleship as the matrix for the constitution of the human person," or a vision of the self that has been "washed out in favor of a more interior (timeless) self-consciousness."[15] Barth is helpful for us in his constant choosing of the former. Barth consistently designates a self that is constituted in the historical action of Jesus and whose inner life is constituted by the Holy Spirit "on the surface" of the self.

Barth discusses the nature of our soul and body near the end of his groundbreaking theological anthropology. In his treatment of "The Creature," in *Church Dogmatics* III/2, Barth reframes the discussion of anthropology in light of Jesus Christ. Having established anthropology in Jesus Christ himself, Barth proceeds to address some problems in the way we think about soul and body. He contends that soul and body must be understood prescriptively in light of the life and history of Jesus. Soul and body must not be construed as self-grounded realities of the creature, as if they are substances within the self, for this leads inevitably to a search for our "inner structure." In contrast to such a construal, Barth draws attention to Jesus, whose life is unified with the work of God. Jesus and his work are one.

> Our starting point, the human nature of Jesus, forbids us at this point to look at any kind of a height selected and adorned by ourselves. Man is from the God who the man Jesus called his Father and whose Son He called Himself. This God as such establishes him as soul and body, constituting the unity and order of this being, and maintaining him in this being in its unity and order. Because He is this God in the constitution of man we have to do with an unshakable but also a saving fact.[16]

Jesus' life is witness to the God who created us living souls by the Spirit. To be created as living souls also means we are created bodies. The Spirit creates soul and body *and* their relation. Through the Spirit, soul and body constitute the one creature; soul and body are two moments of one creaturely reality. By envisioning human life in this way, Barth is trying to avoid a vision of the self with an inner and outer aspect defined respectively as soul and body. Jesus opens the way for an understanding of the unified self, for when we see Jesus' life displayed in scripture, he is not sometimes body and sometimes soul. Jesus acts fully as body and soul. He is "embodied soul" and "besouled body." Barth's odd twist of words highlights his movement away from the idea of a hidden soul in the body.

> [W]hat is there in Him which is only inner and not outer, sensuous and not rational? What does soul or body means for him to the extent that either implies an importance and function of its own, different from and opposed to the other? The Jesus of the New Testament is supremely true man . . . and far from existing as the union of two parts or two "substances," He is one whole man, embodied soul and besouled body: the one in the other and never merely beside it; the one never without the other but only with it.[17]

Because he is the Son of God and the Messiah of Israel, Jesus has the Spirit of God in an absolute sense. But this does not give Jesus' human life a reality different in kind from the rest of us. Rather, the presence of the Spirit in Jesus, the presence of the creative reality of God, reveals the intention of our lives, the order and nature of soul and body. As Jesus has the Spirit, so he lives our reality of soul and body in their designed order.

Barth says that we exist because we have Spirit. The language of "spiritual" structure in Barth is deceptive. He is not saying that we have an inner spiritual reality beneath the flesh or within the body. Rather, he is saying that our lives belong to God and that we cannot know ourselves without God. This self-knowing points to our capability and constant need to hear the word of God. Moreover, Barth considers it insufficient to say that the human spirit (or soul) is simply a relation to God. As a relation that constitutes our lives as creatures, the human spirit is revealed—and in a real sense performed—

by Jesus. God speaks to Jesus, and Jesus is God addressing us. This means that there is no spiritual life, no life in the Spirit, apart from the word of God in Jesus. Of course, what disrupts the speaking of God to us and therefore *disrupts the self* is our sinful lives. To resist the word of God, to refuse to hear it as it is found in Jesus Christ, is to move toward the self-deception that, for Barth, is also death.

> Man has thus to choose between truth and falsehood in his knowledge, and between being and nonbeing in his conduct. The neutrality in which he thinks he can now take himself seriously . . . is quite impossible for him when he is claimed by God. The only choice which now remains for him is to take and conduct himself seriously as a rational being [i.e., a spiritual being], or to fall into complete error in relation both to God and to himself, electing to deny the revelation and will of God and therefore choosing his own nothingness. It can only be a choice between life and death.[18]

Barth locates a word of God outside us that is meant for us and that constitutes our lives. Without the word of God we do not exist. Soul and body, then, are categories of pneumatology; the life of the Spirit, or more precisely the work of the Spirit, is where we locate our inner life. In this sense, Barth's construal of soul and body helps us address the Freud-inspired obsession with the inner life and the imprisoned self. If, as Barth suggests, we are created as those who listen to the word of God, and in this listening understand ourselves as embodied soul and besouled body, then the deception of the self happens in the moments in which soul and body are denied. This denial takes place in the silencing of the word of God meant for our lives.

Barth's construal of soul and body is more involved and complex than I have displayed here. My goal is simply to show how Barth's anthropology resists the kind of interiorizing that shapes so much of our contemporary vision of the inner life. Yet Barth's work builds in subtle ways from the work of Augustine, one of the most important theological voices concerning the inner life. It is to Augustine that I must turn to fill out further the connections between our life in the Spirit and the overcoming of self-deception.

THE SPIRIT AND THE LETTER OF AUGUSTINE

There is a sense in which all of Augustine's work is a fundamental delineation of the overcoming of self-deception.[19] But Augustine also illuminates the relation of the Holy Spirit to the human spirit in a way that holds promise for helping us grasp the connection between self-deception's defeat and the Holy Spirit's continuous claim on our lives. In his fine book *The Darkness of God,* Denys Turner reminds us that "For Augustine, God, self, and interiority all point to one and the same place."[20] Thus, desire has an exterior point or origin:

> In every human desire . . . there is some echo, however
> faint, of God, who in every human desire is in some way
> desired, not necessarily or always *as* God, but always as
> happiness; and true happiness is always in some way
> desired, even happiness sought in false pursuits.[21]

It is a common mistake to view Augustine as the progenitor of an obsessed mentality regarding the inner life. Turner suggests the corrective that Augustine understands interiority to connote both an "ascetical practice" and an "epistemological structure" that form the presupposition of all experience:

> The paradox, then [for Augustine] is that there where
> God is most intimately and subjectively interior to us,
> our inwardness turns out beyond itself toward the eter-
> nal and boundless objectivity of Truth. The language of
> interiority is as it were, self-subverting: the more "inte-
> rior" we are the more our interiority opens out to that
> which is inaccessibly "above" and beyond it.[22]

I quote Turner at length because his corrective captures the incredibly rich soil in which Augustine develops his understanding of the self and the work of the Holy Spirit in our lives.[23] The Spirit's work begins by freeing us from the deception that surrounds us. One of Augustine's most famous works, *The Spirit and the Letter,* gives us a glimpse of the freeing work of the Spirit. This anti-Pelagian text reflects on the book of Romans in order to challenge a vision of the self unaided by the Spirit of grace. The idea of the human will was a primary term of debate in this Pelagian controversy, but Augustine's references to the human will in this text constantly point outward—not to the ability of the will in itself, but to the will of God. Augustine establishes the way he wishes us to understand the working of the will of God in us:

> [T]he human will is divinely assisted to do the right in such manner that, besides man's creation with the endowment of freedom to choose, and besides the teaching by which he is instructed how he ought to live, he receives the Holy Spirit, whereby there arises in his soul the delight in and the love of God, the supreme and changeless Good. This gift is his here and now, while he walks by faith, not yet by sight.[24]

Beyond the important but typical presence of the prevenient grace motif, Augustine does something quite remarkable here. Like an artist, he paints our lives across a broad canvas that encompasses the ability to choose the Good, the instruction in the law, and the gift of the Holy Spirit. The Spirit is decisive for choosing the Good, that is, for doing the will of God. The gift of the Spirit comes to us, drawing us toward our true selves in God. God is the "source of our only real well being."

> Free choice alone, if the way of truth is hidden, avails for nothing but sin; and when the right action and the true aim has begun to appear clearly, there is still no doing, no devotion, no good life, unless it be also delighted in and loved. And that it may be loved, the love of God is shed abroad in our hearts, not by the free choice whose spring is in ourselves, but through the Holy Spirit which is given us.[25]

Augustine maps a pneumatology across our bodies in such a way as to disrupt any sense of an autonomous self, motivated by self-subsisting desires. Specifically, Augustine turns on its head the freedom of choice that he had identified as a creaturely endowment. It is indeed an endowment, but one that needs pneumatological repair and activation.

> Do we then "make void" freedom of choice through grace? God forbid! Yea, we establish freedom of choice. As the law is not made void by faith, so freedom of

> choice is not made void but established by grace. Free-
> dom of choice is necessary to the fulfillment of the law.
> But by the law comes the knowledge of sin; by faith
> comes the obtaining of grace against sin; by the healing
> of the soul comes freedom of choice; by freedom of
> choice comes the love of righteousness; by the love of
> righteousness comes the working of the law.[26]

So, for Augustine, freedom of choice is the capacity to act out of a rightly
ordered will, a will established by a soul that has been healed by the Spirit
of grace. Bound up in this is Augustine's idea that grace is not the denial
of nature but its mending. It is his notion of mending nature that casts
light on the multiple ways Augustine talks about the law of God.

The law is both the moral precepts of the law and the letter of the
law, the scriptures. In both instances, Augustine conceives the work of
the Spirit as inscribing the law on our hearts, and thus effecting a radical reorientation of the location of moral stability in our lives. We
cannot find moral stability through an internal calculus in which we
clarify our motives and desires. Rather, it comes from "outside" us,
from the Spirit who forever inscribes the laws on our hearts. The scriptures do not activate internal spiritual machinery that constructs
moral barriers against the chaos that surrounds us. The law of God
(both as scripture and the moral law) prepares us for the invocation
that is only given by the Christian community in obedience to Jesus:
"Come Holy Spirit, Lord and Giver of life." Only in the invocation,
repeated daily by our lives, may our desires be ordered rightly as those
desires are given by the Spirit of God.

> It follows that the laws of God, written by God himself
> upon the heart, are nothing but the very presence of the
> Holy Spirit who is the finger of God; the presence by
> which charity, the fulness of the law and the end of the
> commandment, is shed abroad in our hearts.[27]

Augustine provides rich resources to aid us in fully recovering a vision
of self-deception and its defeat. Augustine criticizes the Pelagian
image of human life in which human agency is organized through
inner moral commitments, arguing that the inner moral life means
nothing without the working of the Spirit of God. What might we
gain from Augustine as we envision self-deception?

In my view, self-deception begins with a false interiority, a fabricated inner life that carries with it a sense that all the moral resources we need are born out of negotiation with our desires. If I am right that false interiority is the beginning of self-deception, then self-deception must conclude with a misplaced self. This misplaced self "is trapped in the mirror," captivated by its own fabricated image that it believes is progressing toward wholeness.[28] Such an image, created by language, presents a self convinced that emotional health and well-being are achieved by further and further discovery of the inner layers of desire. Yet neither the self nor the image is real, because neither is born of the Holy Spirit.

My construal does not grow from Augustine alone, of course, but also from Barth, with a view toward the seductive power of Freud. In fact, we must come back to Freud, because his more powerful vision of self-deception is yet to be addressed. Freud also understood self-deception as a communal reality, a shared deception that joins individuals to societies and societies to their ancestors. It is this political dimension of self-deception that remains fruitful for social and political criticism, establishing Freud's vision as powerfully attractive. Indeed, this may be Freud's enduring legacy: to teach us to be eternally suspicious of one another, always looking to capture hidden agendas born of unrelenting desires. Only by the operation of suspicion may we uncover the clandestine operations of power and combat the human structures of domination and marginalization.

I believe that Barth and Augustine open a way, however, in which we can address communal self-deception and very real human structures of domination. It is the way of holding one another accountable at the surfaces of life. In face-to-face meeting we can ask the Spirit of God to change us, to mold us into community. We can pray together for the Holy Spirit to free us from inner lies and the captivity of endless self-interpretation, and to fill us with the very desires of God. Self-deception can be overcome only by the overcoming of the self.

I find Barth and Augustine compelling. For both of them, we are not selves at all, but (to use Barth's words) "embodied soul and besouled body," vivified by the Spirit. If we take Barth and Augustine seriously, then we turn Freud's vision on its head and say that the illusion is self-deception. Our response to nontheological conceptions of self-deception is not to dispute them directly, but to disregard them if they require us to enter into a constant interrogation of the self, a cataloging of our authentic desires that are hidden from our thoughts and conduct. We should also disregard them if they tell us to adopt a posture of constant suspicion toward any religious doctrine or practice that seeks to shape the life of a community. For we can know that our spiritual self, and our true selves in community, do not lie not beneath the surface, but in the Spirit.

I conclude with a passage of scripture that was often cited in older dogmatic manuals as a text suggestive of the relation of the Holy Spirit to the human spirit.

> Yet among the mature we do speak wisdom, though it is not a wisdom of this age or of the rulers of this age, who are doomed to perish. But we speak God's wisdom, secret and hidden, which God decreed before the ages for our glory. None of the rulers of this age understood this; for if they had, they would not have crucified the Lord of glory. But, as it is written,
>
> "What no eye has seen, nor ear heard,
>   nor the human heart conceived,
> what God has prepared for those who love him"—
>
> these things God has revealed to us through the Spirit; for the Spirit searches everything [*gar pneuma panta erauna*], even the depths of God [*kai ta batha tou theou*]. For what human being knows what is truly human except the human spirit [*to pneuma tou anthropou*] that is within? So also no one comprehends what is truly God's except the Spirit of God. Now we have received not the spirit of the world, but the Spirit that is from God, so that we may understand the gifts bestowed on us by God. And we speak of these things in words not taught by human wisdom but taught by the Spirit, interpreting spiritual things to those who are spiritual.
>
>   Those who are unspiritual do not receive the gifts of God's Spirit, for they are foolishness to them, and they are unable to understand them because they are spiritually discerned. Those who are spiritual discern all things, and they are themselves subject to no one else's scrutiny.
>
>   1 Corinthians 2:6–15

NOTES

1. Sigmund Freud, *The Future of an Illusion,* trans. W. D. Robson-Scott (New York: W. & W. Norton, 1961). Published as *Die Zukunft einer Illusion,* 1927.

2. Karl Barth, *Church Dogmatics* III/2: §46 (Edinburgh: T. & T. Clark), pp. 344–436.

3. Augustine, *The Spirit and the Letter,* in *Augustine: Later Works,* ed. John Burnaby (Philadelphia: Westminster Press, 1955), pp. 195–250.

4. Paul Ricoeur, *Freud and Philosophy: An Essay on Interpretation* (New Haven, Conn.: Yale University Press, 1970), p. 33. It is important to remember what Ricoeur said in regard to this designation: "These three masters [Marx, Nietzsche, and Freud] of suspicion are not to be misunderstood . . . as three masters of skepticism. They are assuredly, three great 'destroyers.' But that of itself should not mislead us; destruction, Heidegger says in *Sein und Zeit,* is a moment of every new foundation, including the destruction of religion. . . . It is beyond destruction that the question is posed as to what thought, reason, and even faith still signify" (p. 33).

5. Fredric Jameson, *The Political Unconscious: Narrative as a Socially Symbolic Act* (Ithaca, N. Y.: Cornell University Press, 1981). "The center around which the Freudian interpretive system turns is not sexual experience but rather wish-fulfillment, or its more metaphysical variant, 'desire,' posited as the very dynamic of our being as individual subjects" (p. 65).

6. Freud, *Future of an Illusion,* p. 40, emphasis added.

7. Michael Palmer, *Freud and Jung on Religion* (New York: Routledge, 1997), p. 35. See also Merold Westphal, *Suspicion and Faith: The Religious Uses of Modern Atheism* (Grand Rapids: Wm. B. Eerdmans Publishing Co., 1993), pp. 33ff.

8. Freud, *Future of an Illusion,* pp. 65–66.

9. Ibid., p. 67.

10. Ibid., pp. 67–68.

11. Palmer notes the places where Freud's work has been shown to be no longer compelling. See *Freud and Jung,* pp. 60ff.

12. In this way, it could be fruitfully argued that Freud is actually the master of the masters of suspicion. Cf. Julia Kristeva, *New Maladies of the Soul* (New York: Columbia University Press, 1995).

13. Rowan Williams, "The Suspicion of Suspicion: Wittgenstein and Bonhoeffer," in *The Grammar of the Heart: New Essays in Philosophy and Theology,* ed. Richard H. Bell (New York: Harper and Row, 1990), pp. 48–49.

14. I mention this to alert us to the care that must be exercised in referring to a "human spirit" in relation to the Holy Spirit. It is

also important to mention this in order to register some concern about modernity's effect on pneumatology as we move back and forth between ancient and modern regimes of knowledge. In effect, I will assume the correctness of what seems to be a modern configuration—Holy Spirit/human spirit—without accepting any philosophical project for establishing a transcendental humanity. I hope to avoid a theological trajectory that interprets the human spirit as a projection of self-consciousness. I will seek to avoid (and criticize) visions of the human spirit that render the human spirit a constellation of "immortal longings" (to borrow a term from Fergus Kerr).

I am not suggesting by this caution that the idea of a human spirit is a bad one. Rather, I wish to question a procedure that often shows up as a first step in thinking through the Holy Spirit's relation to the human spirit, that is, defining the spiritual essence of being human. This entails establishing the status of the soul in relation to the body or considerations of the relation of soul, spirit, and body with then a fundamental decision made about the exact constitution of soul in relation to body. Certainly, a very important discussion of the immortality of the soul stands as the theological background for this procedure. However, as a first step this procedure becomes a theological cul-de-sac, leaving us engaged in constructions of the human spirit that are deeply individualistic.

15. Mark McIntosh, *Mystical Theology* (Oxford: Basil Blackwell Publisher, 1998), p. 212.

16. Barth, *Church Dogmatics*, III/2, 347.

17. Ibid., 327.

18. Ibid., 423.

19. Jean Bethke Elshtain, *Augustine and the Limits of Politics* (Notre Dame, Ind.: University of Notre Dame Press, 1995). See also John M. Rist, *Augustine: Ancient Thought Baptized* (Cambridge: Cambridge University Press, 1994).

20. Denys Turner, *The Darkness of God: Negativity in Christian Mysticism* (Cambridge: Cambridge University Press, 1995), 55.

21. Ibid., 65.

22. Ibid., 69.

23. Another citation from Turner: "Augustine discovered 'interiority' as such and his own interiority in one and the same act, was startled at once by the novelty and by the continuity of what *his* conversion gave him, wrote *Confessions* at once to *rediscover* and at the same time to *re-create* his own identity and met with all these things in a single 'moment of awe' which fused the conceptual and the experiential in a single experience, the experiential and the conceptual in a single concept." Ibid., 73.

24. Augustine, *The Spirit and the Letter*, 197.
25. Ibid., 197–198.
26. Ibid., 236
27. Ibid., 221.
28. Jacques Lacan, *The Language of the Self: The Function of Language in Psychoanalysis*, trans. Anthony Wilden (Baltimore: Johns Hopkins University Press, 1981). See also V. N. Volosinov, *Freudianism: A Critical Sketch* (Bloomington: Indiana University Press, 1987).

The Trinity and the Christian Life*

Ellen T. Charry

Doctrinal theology and spiritual formation have grown apart over the past millennium. As a theologian, my particular call is to apply the theological tradition—the doctrinal tradition of the church—broadly to the spiritual calling of the Christian life. Here I want to offer some thoughts on how we might apply the church's doctrine of God to daily life.

I am especially comfortable in talking about these things as I stand in a pulpit, next to both the baptismal font and the eucharistic table. Turn your eyes to look at the font filled with water and at the table set with food and drink. Your nurture and nourishment are there, and it is nurture and nourishment by Christian teachings that I want to address.

BEGINNING WITH CHILDREN

An important place to begin is with children, and with our doctrinal heritage in light of the reality of children's lives in American society.

---

*Sections of this address have appeared in *Theology Today*—"Who's Minding the Children?" January 2000, pp. 451–52, and "Spiritual Formation by the Doctrine of the Trinity," October 1997, pp. 367–80—and are reprinted by permission.

Perhaps the most striking parable of childhood in our culture is the animated television show and movie *South Park*. Those who are not familiar with *South Park* may not realize that it is far more than mere entertainment. It is a sadly serious cultural statement in disguise. The film is painfully pointed, and yet understated in certain ways. It is a satire of itself, while simultaneously a satire of the American culture we export all over the globe.

South Park depicts children finding their way in our world with the help of vulgar and socially irresponsible filmmakers, who do not care about them but only about the bottom line. Mothers and teachers are present in the film, but there are no effective fathers in sight. Parents and teachers have scant resources to help children who are being lured by market sleaze, however. All that adults can do is scold and ground their children. At the same time, the adults feel they have to blame someone or something else for luring their children to sneak out to see the sleazy movie. Sadly, the adults are bereft of spiritual resources. Instead of turning toward the children and their spiritual needs, the mothers turn away from them. Rather than nurturing children, mothers choose to make war in order to rid the United States of the corrosive Canadian filmmakers who produced the smutty film that entices their children. Of course, a smutty film is exactly what the "real" film itself is. The film is a film of itself. The medium is the message; the film is a mirror image of ourselves.

The children learn the lessons the adults inadvertently teach, and they also organize to defend their right to the debased entertainment culture that has become their true teacher and parent. In this world there are plenteous genitalia, but no love. There are no role models, but the film includes a vivid portrait of hell, in which we find Gandhi and Martin Luther King Jr. I think John Kennedy is there too, along with Satan and Satan's lover Saddam Hussein. *South Park* has Satan, but no God; hell, but only a heaven depicted as a bevy of naked women; oodles of profanity, but little conversation. Do we have ears to hear and eyes to see?

Although *South Park* is a controversial, challenging, offensive film, it may actually be too easy on us. We see no drugs in the film's world, little violence, no weapons in school. The children give voice to sexually explicit language, but although they are little toilet-mouths they seem to be happy and well adjusted. The corrosive filmmakers turn a profit from the debasement of children, and yet the real lives of children may be far grimmer and more precarious than the filmmakers portray. In the real world of American society, children go to school fearing that they or their friends might not return home at the end of the day. And when they come home, what do too many of them find? Television and Nintendo games. The weakening of marriage and the prevalence of divorce have produced too many single mothers and lost fathers, too many overwhelmed, incompetent parents. Too many children are treated with benign neglect, while others suffer malignant neglect or abuse.

At least the adults in *South Park* are clear that children require both protection and guidance. Even if their efforts on behalf of the children are misguided and ineffectual, the filmmakers portray mothers as loving their children enough to supervise and discipline them. There is a gathering consensus in our culture that the young among us are adrift and in peril. Their self-concept is shaped by entertainment, not the Bible, and they are likely to turn to one another for help rather than to adults. While adults wring their hands, the "market" is giving children role models who are ignoble and a self-concept that is debased. Moreover, the extreme individualism of the culture in which we each pick and choose whatever we want, floating in and out while always laid back, turns the young away from adults and from organized community life that could provide sources of support and structure. Finally, our culture's widespread suspicion of the past and mistrust of institutional life (sanctioned by the church itself) alienates the young from traditional structures of wisdom and safety. There is no reason why youngsters in our culture would think that their parents, or their school, or their church would have anything helpful to offer them.

Churches, schools, and family life alienate the young from themselves while materialism, individualism, and the loss of the past keep the economy booming. The combination is spiritually and physically debilitating for all of us, but especially for children. I suggest that four features of American culture that have developed over the past fifty years have combined to produce this particular combination of debilitating factors for children. I can only name them here.

The first prominent feature of American culture is the post-Freudian, "self" psychology that reached its height in the 1960s. This is the psychology of "*me*," of self-realization and self-actualization, that culminated with Abraham Maslow and Carl Rogers. The second feature is the sexual revolution, which may have been fun for men but has proven problematic for women and disastrous for children. (Actually, even if they have "benefited" by their liberation from responsibilities for women and children, the sexual revolution has proven morally damaging for men as well.) The third feature of American life with negative consequences is the Vietnam War and its aftermath. Vietnam led to loss of respect for leadership and authority. Each person is now assumed to be his or her own ultimate authority on everything. Ambivalence about the very notion of leadership has made it difficult for the clergy, who no longer receive respect for their training or recognition of the authority of their office. These three developments combine with a fourth, which pulls them all together: the entertainment culture.

Focus on self, the sexual revolution, the Vietnam experience, and the entertainment culture combine to create a world in which youngsters are alone and adrift. Adults become intimidated by children, especially teenagers. When children go into their rooms, close their doors, and gaze at their computer screens, too many parents are relieved that they do not have to interact with them. Adults are losing the ability to converse with the young. Perhaps I am overstating the situation, but if so, it is only slightly. The teenage boys who killed and wounded students and teachers at Columbine High School in Colorado are not typical of American youngsters, but they do represent an extreme case of all these features coming together.

BAPTISMAL IDENTITY

What does all this talk about children have to do with Christian theology and Christian doctrine, especially the doctrine of the Holy Spirit in the Trinity? Clearly, contemporary culture gives children a self-concept, a sense of selfhood that is not necessarily healthy. I want to suggest that the Christian tradition has theological resources that we could call on to help protect children from the more debilitating features of the culture. To wit, a God-centered identity can act as an alternative to the entertainment-centered culture of the self that children are given today. When I say "God-centered" identity, I mean a specifically Trinitarian identity. Even more pointedly, a sacrament-expressed doctrine of the Trinity can form persons spiritually, providing a model of self that is an alternative to the culture of "self."

Some Christians have had a radical, forceful conversion experience. But for most people in mainline churches, identification with God comes slowly, and begins at baptism. As we baptize infants we not only proclaim that God-centered Christian identity begins at the font, but also that this identity can be conferred on children without their consent. It is this lack of active assent to baptismal identity that makes the baptism of infants controversial in some circles. In baptizing infants, parents have God imposed on children without their consent, even without their awareness. In bringing their children to the font, parents profess that God is the most worthy object of love there is, for themselves and for their children. Now, I am not so naive that I think everyone who brings a child for baptism realizes that God is the most worthy object of love there is. I realize that many parents do not stop to think about why they bring their children for baptism. Still, they have a right to know what baptism proclaims. They should understand the significance of this dramatic, radical thing that is done to their children when they come to the font. If the church fails to tell parents what we and they are doing, it is remiss.

God gives himself to believers in the waters of baptism and at the table of the Eucharist. The self-giving of God elicits the love that is the beginning of Christian formation. God's self-giving both exemplifies his love and elicits love from us in return: this is the foundation of Christian spiritual growth. Because the Holy Spirit is the one who baptizes, baptism designates persons *for* God, *by* God, in public. In the gathered community, persons are grafted into the divine life.

We often think of Baptism as the rite of welcome into the congregation or even as "joining the church." Such an organizational understanding of baptism has a certain limited validity as a description of sociological reality. But for churches with a theological ecclesiology, Baptism must mean more than being a member of an organization so that Christian identity can function as an alternative to the prevailing culture. Institutional membership alone is insufficient to provide for the spiritual refuge that we and our children need. Sacrament is more than sociology. Baptism by the Holy Spirit into the death of Christ—into the very being of God—is our engrafting into the divine life. In

Baptism, we are sanctified, a reality that is powerfully expressed in the ancient practice of chrismation, sealing with the Holy Spirit by anointing with oil, and so marking the baptized person as Christ's forever. In Baptism we are made holy, consecrated, sanctified, set aside with a special identity grounded in the special claim that God makes on our life.

To be baptized into the name of the Father, and the Son, and the Holy Spirit is to be set into the very center of the Trinitarian life. Thus, a person who knows this, who lives into and out of this baptismal identity, can understand herself as a person enfolded into the life of God. At the mall, in school, on the street, in the church, at home, this baptized one can know that she lives as one who is surrounded by all three Persons of the Trinity on every side. It is precisely that kind of strength and power that children need to wend their way through this often debased, sometimes toxic culture.

Christian identity is neither self-made nor constructed from the narrative of personal history or biology. Christian identity is shaped by the dignity of God, formally bestowed on the whole person by and in the sacrament. In baptism, water is poured over our bodies and the Spirit is poured out on all flesh. Christian theology does not make a distinction between the body and the spirit, for ours is a God who washes and feeds our bodies, who cleanses and nourishes our very selves. Body and soul, the whole person, identified as God's own. This is a cause for great celebration! Baptism can become the drumbeat to which Christians march, the beacon that offers security and hope. Baptism begins a Christian formation in which one is placed under divine guidance and authority, and with which one commits one's self into the care of God, lived out under the care of the believing community. This means that we are never alone, but are always accompanied by the Holy Spirit in the fullness of the Trinity. Baptism sets Christian identity in the Trinity.

TRINITY

Baptism places our identity in Trinity, yet the doctrine of the Trinity is called a mystery. For Christian theology, a mystery is not a secret that we have to discover, or a riddle we have to solve, or a puzzle that we have to unravel. A Christian mystery is not mysterious, but rather an enigma to be dwelt in and savored, a vision of reality that extends beyond our capacity to comprehend. God is both one and three, a complete unity who encompasses internal interdistinctions; this seeming paradox of Trinity is the great mystery of Christian faith. Yet we need not suffer mental gridlock when we dwell within the enigma, for the doctrine of the Trinity has spiritual guidance to offer us and our children.

I want to talk first about simultaneously not knowing and knowing, the paradox of simultaneously not being able to penetrate the mystery and living within the mystery. To say that God in God's self is one substance and yet three Persons is one of the great mysteries of Christian faith. Trying to understand Trinity has been one of the great tasks of doctrinal theology. On one hand, the claim of divine unity and transcendence suggests that God is ordered, settled, and free of the created order. Yet, on the other hand, the claim of divine triplicity suggests that God is active, dynamic, and open to the created order. We cannot resolve this paradox theoretically, but only as God reveals himself in the sending of the Son and the Holy Spirit into the plane of our existence in time and space. This impenetrability of God apart from God's self-giving is a lesson in the humility that is a key element in Christian spiritual development. Christians are baptized into a God whom they cannot fully understand or articulate. However, because modern sensibility craves understanding, the fact that Trinity is not transparent to human intellect has led to Christian embarrassment. This is one reason why Friedrich Schleiermacher and later Paul Tillich put the Trinity at the end of their systematic treatments of theology. The modern mind seeks to know God and to control nature, and so any unknowability regarding God is taken as an insult to the modern scientific imperative. Yet the very reality of God escapes us if we first rebuff the impenetrable wall that painfully separates us from the source of our own life. The very elusiveness of God's inner reality that makes us dependent on revelation reinforces the teaching of Genesis 3 that we cannot and should not have all the knowledge and control we crave.

In theory, the secular self knows no limits. Human ingenuity sallies forth with the entrepreneurial spirit that desires to extend medical technology indefinitely and that assumes social policy and engineering will bring all human problems under control. But human ingenuity stops at the door of the Trinity. The doctrine of the

Trinity injects a note of tentativeness, hesitation, even incompetence deep within our being. In the presence of divine mystery we cannot stand on our own feet and presume to master the source of our life. Anxiety about our ignorance in the face of the divine opacity of the Trinitarian mystery is a moment of self-knowledge, however, and a truly Christian one at that. It speaks haltingly of human limitation, of human dependency, not glibly in words that trip lightly off the modern tongue. We need the divine mystery to keep our modesty and humility alive so that we may tread God's earth gently, continuously reminded that we are not the world's owners, but only the stewards of God's creation. At the baptismal font it is clear that we do not even own ourselves. There is a transcendent reality that we cannot, and for our own good must not, try to penetrate. We can only stand before the mystery in humble obedience and gratitude. The Trinitarian mystery exposes a cognitive concupiscence in human nature that the maturing Christian can turn to spiritual advantage. As Trinity confronts us with our inappropriate curiosity, we may be encouraged to question other aspects of the human project. Are our undertakings important or frivolous, advantageous or harmful? Who benefits and who loses?

Although it may be a cultural heresy, I suggest that humility and intellectual insecurity would serve us well in the field of medical technology. The capabilities of medical technology, combined with our desire to put off death as long as possible, are creating monsters in our midst that we do not know how to control. The mystery of the Trinity that confronts the baptized forces believers to ask what we really need to know about life and death, and what we really need to do in the face of life and death—what medical possibilities may be potentially harmful to us even though we have access to technology that may accomplish them. Is it possible for us to turn away from what it is possible for us to do? In light of the moral ambiguities now emerging from medical technology and its cultural companions, we should welcome Trinity's check on our cognitive concupiscence, for it offers to inject spiritual considerations into what threatens to become a frenetic reflexive existence that cannot see beyond financial or other short-term considerations.

Suggesting that there are areas into which we should not venture appears to be a constraint on human freedom. Yet it identifies precisely the realm of Christian freedom in which the believer is freed from enslavement to the expectations of the culture. What would our society look like if, together with artistic self-expression and entrepreneurial freedom, we also asked what God would have us create, discover, and express?

KNOWING AND LOVING

The mystery of the Trinity may chasten our curiosity, yet its effect on us is also troubling. Saint Augustine was plagued by the problem of knowing and not knowing throughout his life. He wanted to love God completely, but he was puzzled by how he could love what he did not know. Augustine wanted to know God, not in order to gain the power over others that knowledge brings, but in order to gain power over himself. Augustine exhibits the proper function of knowledge. Thus, beyond humility, the second spiritual gift of the Christian teaching about the triune God is to show us the spiritual value of knowing. Augustine never understood the inner life of God. In particular, he did not understand the place of the Holy Spirit within the Trinity. That is a pretty big omission for the most influential mind in Christian history! His unknowing did not plague him, however, because he sought a different kind of knowledge.

One of Augustine's recurring themes is that we can use the material things of creation to learn God's wisdom. As we learn of God's goodness from God's actions, we may infer what the church fathers haltingly called "the divine essence." Knowing the story of God's dealings with us in creation, we are given spiritual knowledge of the wisdom, the goodness, the truth, and the moral beauty that is the very being, the *ousia* of God. By knowing and loving the beauty and goodness of our God, and by yearning to know God more fully, our desires are already oriented in a godly and noble manner. We may come to taste, to touch, to dwell in the wisdom of God, which is the patrimony of our baptism. Thus, the Christian gradually comes to love and enjoy the wisdom that is God even though the precise interrelationships of the three Persons of the Trinity may escape her or him. Augustine understood that wisdom is spiritually superior to correct information, for it uplifts the knower, bringing one into intimate contact with the known. Augustine urges Christians to love God's beauty and good-ness, known in the saving wisdom of Christ on the cross and in the sanctifying power of the Holy Spirit. By loving God on the basis of knowledge given in revelation, we become conformed to God, for we become what we know as the object of our love. Children become what they know when they see *South Park,* but Christians have an alternative. We can know the goodness of God and, in knowing, become assimilated to what we know. Knowing by loving assumes that we infer God's wisdom and goodness from God's works.

The notion of knowledge through love has been roundly attacked in modernity, beginning with David Hume in the eighteenth century. Since then, modernity has assumed that we cannot know God from the world or from God's preachers. But I think this was a mistake. Today it is possible to reclaim softly the notion that we can know the goodness of God. We are not trying to know the concrete material reality of God, of course; we are seeking to know the spiritual reality of God. It is possible in postmodernity to recover knowledge of God that modernity has told us is off limits to us. Hume's challenge may have set Christian theologians on a dubious digression, for it is impor-tant that we remain connected with the reality that we *can* know God.

FATHER, SON, AND HOLY SPIRIT

Thus far I have talked about the spiritual-forming power of the unity of God, the oneness of God. Now I would like to turn to the divine triplicity, the claim that God's being is expressed in three Persons, or three energies, or three identities. This is summarized for us in the creedal affirmations that God is Father, Son, and Holy Spirit. The Nicene and Apostles' Creeds associate creation with the Father, salva-tion with the Son, and sacraments, scripture, and eschatological hope with the Spirit. In expressing Christian trust that life, salvation, and new life come from God, and that they are extended in differentiated ways, the creeds refer Christian experience of God to intrinsic distinc-tions within God's being. This eternal self-differentiation suggests the image of a blastula, an enclosure of divine energy that awaits the appro-priate moment of actualization. Opening like petals of a flower in acts of judgment and mercy, encouragement and hope—all for us through the bestowal of spiritual gifts—God discloses himself as Lord and Savior of all creation. The teaching of the eternal self-differentiation of God is replete with the energy of the divine work. God is all that is needed for the redemption of the cosmos. The very being of God anticipates being with us and for us in creation, in the history of Israel, in Jesus Christ, and in the Spirit-given life of the church.

Envisioning the divine triplicity graphically may be helpful, but as soon as we speak of eternal self-differentiation in terms of blastulas and flowers we have already fallen into the error of concrete thinking that Saint Augustine labored so arduously to release us from. On this model, we might think of God as a thing alongside other things, and we would be distracted from the wisdom, truth, and beauty of God that is our true focus. The Trinitarian doctrine of God begs for analogies and graphic representation, but as soon as we start down that road we risk being sidetracked, diverted from the wisdom of God that is our proper goal and the love of God that is our true liberation. So we must take a step back from analogies and models in order to move toward their purpose.

What, then, is the spiritual guidance offered by a God who is three in one and one in three? How are we to live with the God who is revealed to us from the beginning as Father, Son, and Holy Spirit? We have already seen that baptism anchors Christian identity in the being of God, thereby offering us protection from our self-constructed identities. The enigmatic nature of the Trinity both checks cogitative concupiscence and provides a name for ultimate truth and goodness. Now we can begin to understand how the divine triplicity further strengthens our theological identity.

Scriptural precedent and pastoral practice have assigned to each of the three "hypostases" specific responsibilities for creation. This functional differentiation indirectly tells us something about ourselves as well as about God. God is so concerned for the flourishing of creation that the divine triplicity itself is for the sake of the creation's flourishing. The being of Father, Son, and Holy Spirit as creator, redeemer, and sanctifier suggests that humankind needs more than simply to be created and then set on its way. Thus, Trinity reveals that God's own being is structured around our needs. That the Son and Spirit are indeed God, and are sent into the world to repair and sanctify us, brings us face to face with our need for precisely the work that God does. We need to be confronted by our sin in the cross of Christ, and offered the hope of forgiveness in his resurrection. We need to be sealed with the power of the Holy Spirit for new life in Christ, and gifted with capacities for love of neighbor and service to others in the upbuilding of the entire body. Son and Spirit are not afterthoughts, self-differentiations of God undertaken after the Fall to close the barn door after the horse is out. Christians understand Father, Son, and Holy Spirit as coeternally God.

The great debates of the fourth century concluded that the divine triplicity anticipates the full force of human need from eternity. Creation, redemption, and sanctification together are God's plan for us, and the triune God is perfectly constituted to actuate that plan. The divine persons hold creation, redemption, and sanctification together eternally. Perhaps God understands us better than we understand ourselves by anticipating our need for rescue, purification, and new life. If we recognize the divine triplicity as an opportunity to understand God's perception of our own needs, we become better able to distinguish genuine need from artificially or commercially manufactured need. We become able to act effectively on God's understanding of our needs while recognizing the falsehood of culture's constructed needs. The divine hypostases, employed in human history, are the means of our true happiness. With the Trinity as a guide to our own needs, we encounter a plumb line that clears our minds and focuses our energies so that we are able to distinguish pursuits that ennoble us from pursuits that harm ourselves or others. We learn from the anticipated work of the three Persons of the Trinity, discovering what it is that we truly need. In the process, we become more mature, better able to judge the culture that claims us so that we can claim God as the true center of our lives.

The divine triplicity is also pastorally helpful in the face of the stresses of modern life. The frenetic pace of life with its multiple roles and demands makes its difficult to hold together our varied obligations nobly. Jobs, family, and our obligations as consumers pull us in multiple directions. The demands of business require attitudes and values and skills that are different from those required to mind children or find our way through the maze of society's amusements and products. One can become frazzled, spiritually disheveled, in trying to maintain a coherent self. It may even be tempting for us to cultivate different personae for each sphere of life. One may be hard-nosed at work, gentle at home, carefree at play. In the midst of this unrelenting pressure, the divine Trinity offers a vision of concrete wholeness and wholesomeness. The variegated work of the divine hypostases delimit the single work of God. In the doctrine of the Trinity we have a unified theological framework that knits together what can so easily become conflicting goods in our own lives. If the divine triplicity is for our well-being, then the various divine works display a coherent purpose and a standard of goodness in God that can become a guide for all the personae that we cultivate in all the various roles we play. Trinity is a unifying model for our self-integration. We can learn stability from God when we cannot discern it in the various tugs and pulls on our identity. The conjoint work of redeeming, sanctifying, and guiding, then, is a centripetal dynamic to counter the centrifugal forces of modern life.

Finally, accepting God's exalted purpose for the whole cosmos as our own purpose discloses the theological link between our own goals and endeavors and the goals and endeavors of others who stand on the same Trinitarian foundation. Whether or not those with whom we are linked recognize this common ground, and whether or not they recognize their own grounding in the Trinity, is irrelevant. Believers are implicated in the well-being of others because of God's redemptive destiny for the entire cosmos. All persons participate in God's redemptive destiny by virtue of their creation in the image of God. Christians participate specifically and explicitly by virtue of their baptism. Because the triune life of God encompasses salvation within itself, all of the baptized are taken up into the divine work of the cosmos's redemption. One's behavior as a spouse, a parent, a worker, a supervisor, a citizen, and a consumer are all located in the midst of God's plan for redemption of the cosmos. One is never acting alone on one's own behalf in any sphere of life. One's goals are taken up into God's goals, so that one's life bears responsibility for its contribution to the flourishing of all creation. The redemptive purpose of God for us enables us to align ourselves with the divine purpose freely, and to realize that in the act of attending to God we are cooperating with our own true happiness.

I have argued that the doctrine of the Trinity provides Christians with the knowledge of God that elicits the love and trust that create a *theological* identity and purpose, and thus provides a godly standard of coherent living that can guide intelligible, stable, and properly happy Christian living. Knowing and loving God the Holy Trinity is genuinely salutary for people because people truly need God. A pastoral examination of the doctrine of God assumes that the triune God of Christian faith provides an entrée to a happy and productive life that can address spiritually the negative effects of contemporary life.

The Christian doctrinal exegesis that I am suggesting may be undertaken so that we see God more clearly, love God more dearly, and follow him more nearly, day by day. This is especially apparent when we come to this Table where we take the very being of God into ourselves for our nourishment. As we are fed, we know whose we are and who we are, and so our identity is reconsolidated. The triune identity is a shield and a refuge, a compass to direct us as we wend our way through this culture, cleansed and nourished by the sacraments, and supported by all other faithful Christians in the church.

The Holy Spirit and Spiritual Formation

Elizabeth Nordquist

I am a Presbyterian pastor, a teacher of Christian spirituality in a Presbyterian Seminary, a spiritual director, and most importantly, a person who continues to recognize that my life is being formed and transformed by the Holy Spirit, the presence and energy of the risen Christ who lives in me. The risen Christ lives in my body, in my spirit, in my person, as well as in everyone who calls Jesus Christ "Lord." My hope now is to reflect on the meaning of our doctrine of the Holy Spirit for the lives of persons and the life of our community.

MEMORIES AND HOPES

I confess that I did not know much about the Holy Spirit when I was young, even though I grew up in a devout family with an eclectic assortment of theological roots from various Protestant traditions. I recognized that the Holy Spirit rounded out the Trinity, and that the Holy Spirit was always mentioned in the benediction at the conclusion of worship. As a teenager, I learned the chorus "Spirit of the living God, fall afresh on me," and I loved what its simple phrases and harmonies suggested about closeness to God. That song resonated with my longings for God, longings that I could not always name.

Whatever formal teaching I had about the Holy Spirit in Sunday school or in youth group has passed out of memory. But as a junior at U.C.L.A., I was confronted with a group of Christians who seemed to know everything there was to know about the Holy Spirit. Their Holy Spirit was something or someone who came in extraordinary experiences that empowered people to do exotic things like speaking in tongues and casting out demons. All of this was shocking to me and to my pietistic, rather staid family. I wondered whether or not this Holy Spirit was related to the one in the benediction at the end of worship.

At the same time I was completely convinced of the value of the education and spiritual nurture I had received as a Christian young person. I continued to believe that if I observed all the prescribed disciplines of Bible study, prayer, tithing, and sharing my Christian faith, God would be pleased, I would know more about God, and I would be acceptable within the Christian community. As I became an adult, however, some of my certainty about the efficacy of those disciplines came into question. To begin with, I saw that some of my peers, who were as faithful or more faithful than I in observing those spiritual practices, became lost. They were lost to the church, and often to themselves. I wondered if God thought they were lost too. I also noticed that even among those who continued to observe the Christian practices that we shared, there was tremendous variety in the way they lived out their faith. Equally faithful practice led to different callings, different denominations, different points of view, and different styles of life. There had to be more to spiritual formation than simply observing a set of disciplines.

I have come to understand that the formation of a Christian is the work of the Holy Spirit, the Lord, the giver of life. The Holy Spirit is the continuing energy of God in Jesus Christ, who lives in the individual believer, is present when Christ's people gather, and inhabits all of creation. It is that same Holy Spirit, whose description had frightened me as a college junior, whom I have come to know and understand more fully as the one who powerfully connects faithful practices of Christian discipleship to the whole person. This Holy Spirit brings about internal transformation and empowers people to respond to Christ's call to go out and to serve the world. This Holy Spirit, always present in our life by virtue of our baptism, is God with us, God in us. I now understand that the closeness to God that was so winsome to me when I sang, "Melt me, mold me, fill me, use me," was a prayer that was being answered even as I voiced it. I have also come to know that the Holy Spirit's freedom forms people into Christ's image in a limitless variety of ways. Thus, Christian sisters and brothers become more of who each one in particular was meant to be as the Spirit works in each person.

What surprised me when I became a pastor was that few church folk in our tradition knew what to think about the Holy Spirit. Of course, if their early religious imprinting was as vague as mine had been, I should not have been surprised at all. Sometimes I felt as if I were in first-century Ephesus with the apostle Paul when new disciples said, "We have not even heard that there is a Holy Spirit" (Acts 19:2). There is a communication block in our conversations about the Holy Spirit, a barrier that may be located in our vocabulary. Different traditions have used different words to describe the ways human beings are shaped by the presence of the Holy Spirit in their lives. We talk about discipleship, Christian nurture, the pursuit of holiness, spirituality, and our Reformed term "piety" (a word that has taken on unfortunate pejorative connotations in North American culture). It may be valuable and important for us to be in conversation with other Christians to discover the rich variety of understandings about the work of the Holy Spirit in the life of the believer and the life of the community of faith.

A deeper problem than vocabulary, however, is the seeming lack of awareness that many church members have about the presence and the power of the Spirit in their own lives. Sadly, I hear over and over again from church folk that the church has not been a place where spiritual questions can be asked, let alone unanswered. Far too often, we have failed to provide adequate guidance, to make our tradition's theology accessible, and to provide sacred time and space for church members to experience what it means to live a life that is attentive and responsive to the energetic and comforting presence of God the Spirit.

CHURCH AND CULTURE

At the same time that some parts of our church languish in their awareness and understanding of the Holy Spirit, there is a cultural groundswell of interest in a generic spirituality and a fascination with the plethora of particular spiritualities from around the world. When the Dalai Lama came to Los Angeles at the same time that Bruce Springsteen appeared for a concert, members of the press were placing odds on who would draw the bigger crowd. The media were baffled by the Dalai Lama's popularity with the large number of people who came to his appearances, from many religious traditions. Christians and Jews as well as Buddhists flocked to hear him, and they left feeling inspired and blessed. Some reported sensing holiness in his presence, or peacefulness, or a connection to ultimate meaning. It is tragic that many of these seekers had been part of the church yet had not found there anything that spoke to their longings for holiness, for peace, for meaning, for connection to the mystery of the Other.

The convergence of our need as a church and the needs of the culture invite us to address the very questions that are under consideration in this convocation: Who is this Holy Spirit? How does the Spirit connect us to the risen Christ? What do we teach about the Holy Spirit in the church? How can we provide opportunities for people to be transformed by the Spirit's presence in their lives? The Presbyterian Church (U.S.A.) has responded in important ways to these needs during the last decade. Our General Assembly program now includes an Office of Spiritual Formation, and many individual congregations provide creative opportunities for spiritual growth. Theological seminaries are responding to the needs of their students and of the church by instituting formal academic concentrations in Christian spirituality and by providing focused opportunities for students to integrate spiritual awareness and practice into their studies and lives. Attention that must be paid is being paid.

The spiritual formation of Christians is a central part of our tradition. John Calvin's magnificent chapter on faith in the *Institutes* includes a wonderful section on the Spirit's role in sealing faith in our hearts:

> It now remains to pour into the heart itself what the mind has absorbed. For the Word of God is not received by faith if it flits about in the top of the brain, but when it takes root in the depth of the heart that it may be an invincible defense to withstand and drive off all the stratagems of temptations. . . . The spirit accordingly serves

as a seal, to seal up in our hearts those very promises the
certainty of which it has previously impressed on our
minds; and takes the place of a guarantee to confirm and
establish them.[1]

For Calvin, a Christian is formed as the word of God descends from
the mind to the heart, and is sealed there by the Holy Spirit. Even so,
difficulty remains for some of us, for we feel that we are

standing in the mystery
on holy ground
in sacred space
    where the Spirit-wind blows where it will
    where the Spirit is free
        free to teach people the truth as Jesus as promised
        free to correct and to convict of sin
        free to comfort and to heal
        free to call and to send
        free to shape each person uniquely
        through words, images, sensations, and experiences.

We cannot accurately chart or predict what the Spirit of God will do
in each person, in each fellowship, in each part of the world. The part
of us that likes order more than the unpredictable movement of the
Spirit may find this troubling, because spiritual formation is not
quantifiable, not easily analyzed, not reducible to a set of disciplines,
and, as the Pentecost Christians in Jerusalem discovered, not easily
contained.

Perhaps we are afraid of the caricatures of the emotional spirituality portrayed on television or in the movies. We may be afraid that
attention to spiritual growth means leaving our intellects behind in
order to get in touch with feelings . . . or even to manufacture them.
We may even fear that giving attention to our inner selves will siphon
energy from our responsibility to do acts of justice and mercy in the
church and the world. Perhaps we think we will lose our privacy if we
are asked to reveal our spiritual journey to others, or even that we will
suffer the judgment of others if we are rated unspiritual or spiritual in
the wrong way. All these fears are real, but we must face them and risk

attention to this spiritual journey. To refuse the risk of creating space for our spiritual formation means quenching the Holy Spirit, diminishing the Spirit's power and energy in the church and its members, truncating the mission and ministry of God's people in the world. God has not given a spirit of fear. God invites us into a pilgrimage of growth in the grace and knowledge of Jesus Christ, which is facilitated, energized, and effected by the Holy Spirit.

SPIRITUAL FORMATION AND THE CHURCH

The institutions of the church bear responsibility for making spiritual formation possible in the lives of believers. I once heard a seminary president answer a question about the school's responsibility for the spiritual growth of students by saying that the seminary had a different mandate, and that it was the students' responsibility to take care of their own journeys with the Spirit. While I agree that each Christian chooses how to respond or not to respond to the activity of the Spirit, I also believe that our institutional church life can either encourage and enrich our spiritual formation, or block and hinder it. Amish quilt makers often leave one block or square unfinished, thus creating a space for the Spirit. We have to create space for the Spirit in the lives of our institutions.

Our tradition creates space for spiritual formation in corporate worship. As the primary gathering of the church, worship provides opportunity to preach the word, to thank God, to confess sin and receive forgiveness, to intercede for others, and to offer ourselves in wonder, love, and praise. We must be vigilant, however, to ensure that our services of worship avoid two pitfalls. First, whether it is formal or informal, liturgy is the work of people, not the preserve of pastors, musicians, and other religious professionals. When the people of God gather to worship, those who are responsible for designing and facilitating worship must pay attention to the architecture of the service, the syntax of response and prayer, the rhythm of activity and contemplation. These elements of worship provide space for the Spirit to connect mind and heart, hearing and reflecting, learning and trusting. Second, we must remain clear that worship is not entertainment. Kierkegaard reminds us that the congregation is not an audience whom we try to please or to whom we pander. God is the audience, and the congregation is the acting troop. Therefore, the liturgical choices we make must serve the Word—Jesus Christ—in scripture, sermon, and sacraments. Worship design and leadership should create space where the Spirit can move freely to form the congregation in Christ's image.

A second goodly heritage of the Reformed tradition is a commitment to theology and the life of the mind. I am grateful to be part of a church that knows theology matters, and that embeds that commitment in educational requirements for its leaders and educational opportunities for its members. However, we have become aware that pedagogy—our methods of teaching—is as important as the theology we teach. Gone is the era of teaching in which an expert pours information into a learner. We know that learners must have the opportunity for data to simmer, for them to interact with information and to question interpretations, before it becomes their own. The educational commitment of our church's institutions must include pedagogies that give space for the Word to flourish in the heart of seekers.

Worship and education are classic church practices in the Reformed tradition. We have supported them more or less faithfully throughout our history. But our institutions have other responsibilities as well.

OPENING THREE WINDOWS

We can open three windows. First, we can open a window onto a clear space and free time in which our formation by the Spirit can take place. These spaces and times are something other than the multiplicity of programs and activities that fill up the church calendar. Church programs often contribute to our chronic busyness, encouraging the faithful only in workaholic sin. Proliferation of programs without consideration of their impact on the souls of church members crowds out time for recollecting the goodness of God, for reflecting on the mystery of faith, and for discerning the leading of the Spirit. I do not know what time frame John Calvin had in mind as he envisioned the Word descending to take root in the heart, but I suspect it did not occur in a hectic rush. As a Presbyterian interested in spiritual formation said to me recently, "Holiness takes time." We need to create time and space in services of worship, in committee agendas, in the congregation's annual calendar, when people are invited to set themselves apart to rest for a while with the risen Christ. Where in the rhythm of our church life do our leaders observe Sabbath? Where can a person ask the questions about the Spirit that stir in mind and heart and soul?

In addition to creating time and space, we are also called to open windows onto attitudes of attentive listening to the Spirit. From Christian contemplative traditions through the ages (and some traditions that are not Christian), we learn the value of attentiveness and awareness. From Elijah who heard the sound of sheer silence against the backdrop of meteorological pyrotechnics, to Jesus who retreated to the hills after ministry among the crowds, we see the importance of attentive listening for the Word of God, the sounds of the Spirit of God among us. Silence, solitude, meditation on scripture, and contemplation of the presence of God all have biblical precedents, and all allow the Spirit room to move, shape, inspire, and direct.

As a teacher in the program of Christian spiritual formation at San Francisco Theological Seminary, I can observe the evolving work of my colleagues Mark Yaconelli and Andy Dreiser, who head the Youth Ministry and Spirituality Project. The three-and-a-half-year research project is designed to develop a contemplative model of youth ministry for use in Christian congregations. In sixteen pilot churches, youth ministry teams of adults and youth begin the process by praying together. Prior to any program visioning or planning, the team prays and waits to see what God is leading them to do. Reports from the churches vary widely, but the question for each of them and for us is how we can learn to listen for the Spirit's direction. Where are the places in our personal and corporate lives that we listen for the Spirit? How do we discern the Spirit together so that we come to a consensus that leads to decision?

The window onto open space and free time and the window onto attentive listening may give us the daring we need to open a window onto the possibility of spiritual friends. Seekers often need to be connected with people who can be spiritual friends or companions with them on their journeys, sharing the realities and perplexities of the pilgrimage. We are not called to follow Christ in solitary isolation. In Celtic Christian traditions, every person was to have a soul friend— an *anam chara*. The soul friend was one with whom to trade confidences, exchange dreams, and share longings, a confidant who could be trusted with one's faith journey. Classical definition of a pastor used to include the calling to be a spiritual guide to parishioners. But now, the job description for many pastors is weighed down with accretions from loud and demanding disciplines: chief executive officer . . . community organizer . . . fund-raiser . . . therapist—all in addition to preacher, teacher, and pastoral visitor. Although being a spiritual friend certainly should be part of the pastoral vocation, pastors in most churches cannot be an intensive, extended spiritual friend to each member of the congregation. That is why some Protestants are beginning to reclaim the ancient practice of spiritual direction. Several Presbyterian seminaries have instituted programs to train spiritual directors, persons who come alongside of another to reflect, listen, pray, and discern what the Spirit is doing. Spiritual directors are partners on the spiritual journey.

A painting by Raphael in the Prado in Madrid is an icon of what spiritual companionship is. It is a painting of the visitation, the meeting of mothers-to-be Mary and Elizabeth. The two are embracing, for together they have discerned the working of the Holy Spirit in ways they could not have understood individually. In this Gospel scene, we see what spiritual direction is like. We all need other people in our lives, perhaps especially in our spiritual lives. There are many models of spiritual direction, for there is no formula to be followed. Spiritual Directors International, an ecumenical confederation of Christians called to that ministry, is a resource that identifies and supports people in the development of their local ministries. In spite of our North American propensity for rugged individualism, we know that we human beings are made in God's image for companionship and friendship, and that the Spirit often speaks and prompts us through others.

John Calvin reminds us that "we need outward helps to beget and increase faith within us, and advance it to its goal."[2] Now, he had in mind pastors and teachers of the church, and I agree, but I would add that our churches also have a responsibility to help members find others who will be companions on the inner way. Who are the people in our congregations whose spiritual formation is a model for others? Who has the gifts of listening and noticing the movement of the Spirit? Who prays discerningly for others and with others?

I believe it is important that our church's leaders—ministers of Word and Sacrament, elders, and deacons—have spiritual friends as much as anyone in the church. Spiritual formation and transformation are ongoing processes. How easy it is in the life of the everyday pastor to be choked by the tyranny of the urgent, to be isolated by loneliness at the top, running on empty because all energy has been used up in caring for the flock. Some pastors find friendship and affirmation in pastors' groups, folks just like themselves. But even there, competition, lack of truth telling, and fear of failure clog the open space of collegiality, unless intentional commitment is made to keep space clear for observing and trusting the movement of the Holy Spirit. As church institutions we must organize our ministries so that the ongoing spiritual formation of our leadership it is not just an afterthought, something that has to be squashed in to an already full calendar, but something that we value and seek and plan for and pray for, as we order our common life.

A JOURNEY OF THE SPIRIT

What can we expect if we embark on an intentional journey of the Spirit? What can we tell others to expect? There are some things that we should expect to expect. First of all, we should anticipate that spiritual formation is a lifelong process. Holiness does take a long time, for we are being transformed from glory to glory. We also should anticipate that when we attend to our spiritual journey we will come to know more about the triune God and the way God's Holy Spirit works in us and the world. We should also expect to know more about ourselves. Because the Spirit gives particular gifts to particular people for particular tasks, we will know more about the gifts we have been given . . . and which ones we have not been given. We will also know our sin. To know ourselves it not an end in itself, but rather an act of faith for God's glory, an enhancement of our capacity to respond to the call of the Holy Spirit in our lives, so that we may pour ourselves out for God's sake and the sake of the world.

When we attend to our spiritual journeys, we will become better able to discern the Spirit's call and to receive the resources that the Spirit provides to respond to that call. It is important to acknowledge that we will not always feel great. In fact, some days will leave us feeling worse than when we began. A person with whom I am working said he had thought that if he started on a spiritual journey his life would be happy, but that there were times when he felt more miserable than when he began. It is true enough that some days are like that, but those feelings are never a sign that the Spirit has abandoned us. The Holy Spirit is present in our times of weakness and places of darkness.

It is also important to say that the spiritual journey is not only for introverts or for the socially inept. All are invited to participate in the Spirit's work. It is the call to God's people of every personality type, and all of us discover that the Spirit appears in surprising places. The Holy Spirit is present in the ordinary and familiar, as well as on the mountaintop. The Spirit is present in the mundane as well as in moments of ecstasy. The Spirit blows powerfully and unpredictably, but surely the Spirit's wind and fire form in us the good fruit that is the sign of the Spirit's presence in our life.

I recently received a phone call informing me of the death of a young woman with whom I have worked for over ten years. She would have been thirty-three years old last Monday, and I grieved along with others around the country who had invested in her, who had loved her in an amazing way. When she came to us she presented a challenge that was beyond our human expertise. She had been sexually abused in her family and spiritually abused in a cult. She suffered from a self-destructive eating disorder. The people of the community of faith who gathered around her tried to put themselves in the space where the Spirit would teach us and equip us to respond to a young woman's howling need. Over weeks and months we were able to arrange for hospitalization and psychiatric care, then to provide housing and reparenting to give her all the things she had been deprived of in her early years. We prayed for her and with her. We established a contingency fund for the time when she would become more self-reliant. Throughout it all, we tried to be faithful in friendship. Slowly, over time, profound healing took place. Even though deep scars remained, her transformation was miraculous. And then she died of a blood clot that was thrown randomly as she was walking her dog. No one knows why. Yet what happened in her and in us was transformational. Even as we mourn her death we rejoice in the work of God's Holy Spirit in her all-too-brief life, and we celebrate what happened in our lives as the Spirit worked in us through her.

It was the work of the Spirit in her and in us, so we live in freedom even as we mourn, because we participated in the work of the Spirit, the Lord and Giver of life. Lisa is free, and we are free to know ourselves forgiven for the things we did and the things we neglected to do. We are free to remember with gratitude the work of the Spirit in us, bearing fruit that we knew we were incapable of producing. To experience the Holy Spirit's Christian formation in us is to live in freedom and witness good fruit in our lives. May God grant us the grace to bear fruit and to live as free people. Amen.

NOTES

1. John Calvin, *Institutes of the Christian Religion,* Library of Christian Classics, ed. John T. McNeill, trans. Ford Lewis Battles (Philadelphia: Westminster Press, 1960), 3.2.36.
2. Ibid., 4.1.1., p. 1011.

PROCLAMATION
Four sermons preached
at the convocation

It's Not about You

M. Craig Barnes

So then, brothers and sisters, we are debtors, not to the flesh, to live according to the flesh—for if you live according to the flesh, you will die; but if by the Spirit you put to death the deeds of the body, you will live. For all who are led by the Spirit of God are children of God. For you did not receive a spirit of slavery to fall back into fear, but you have received a spirit of adoption. When we cry, "Abba! Father!" it is that very Spirit bearing witness with our spirit that we are children of God, and if children, then heirs, heirs of God and joint heirs with Christ— if, in fact, we suffer with him so that we may also be glorified with him.

Romans 8:12–17

I don't remember when I first heard the phrase "It's not about you," but I really like it . . . a lot. I have yet to find a pastoral situation in which it is not relevant.

When someone comes to see me for the fiftieth time to talk about all the hurt they received from their family of origin, after all the careful listening and responsible counsel, I eventually have to say, "Hey, it wasn't about you. They were just too hurt themselves."

On those terrible nights when I am stuck in a committee meeting that is going south in a hurry, it's usually because someone is far too invested with a personal agenda. It doesn't help matters to keep arguing the issue on the table, because that's not what is driving the debate. It's more helpful to look at the complainer and gently say, "You know, this really isn't about you."

And weddings? Oh, the phrase is perfect for weddings. The bride and groom are standing in front of everyone—looking better than they are ever going to look again—getting all the attention, too many presents, and so much affirmation. It would be easy to think that this *is* about each of them. Nope. Just look at their worn-out parents sitting in the front pew. They understand that marriage is never just about you.

Even when I am sitting by the hospital beds of those who are dying, it is important that I, at least, know this most intimate of all events is not really about them. It is about the God who created and sustained them, and is now bringing them home.

As our Confessions remind us, it is always about God. The reason biblical faith makes praising God its central goal is not because God is insecure and needs lots of affirmation, but because the Bible is concerned that we enjoy the freedom in knowing "it's not about us." If it is always about God, then we are free from the burden of pretending to be gods. Instead, we can return to our mission of witnessing to the grace God is giving us.

When we come to the Lord's Table to have our faith nurtured, we must be careful to remember that the sacrament proclaims that even our faith is not really about us. It isn't about our personal relationship to God. This Table claims that our faith is about the Son's relationship with his Father, into which the Holy Spirit adopts us, making us heirs of God and joint heirs with Christ. According to Paul, this gives us the freedom also to cry out, "Abba! Father!" "For all who are led by the Spirit of God are children of God. For you did not receive a spirit of slavery to fall back into fear, but you have received a spirit of adoption."

If you do not feel like the beloved child of God, the challenge is not to try to concoct emotions with the aid of sentimental worship, which is just another way of making worship about you. No, the challenge is to come to the objective material reality of this Table, where we are met by the Spirit of God, who leads us to our place at the family table. The Reformed tradition has always asserted that the place where Christ is present is not in the elements—not in, with, over, or under—not even at the table. Jesus Christ is risen and is now at the right hand of the Father. It is the Holy Spirit who meets us here and lifts us up to take our place in the holy community of the Trinity. We receive this not because we deserve it, but because we need it.

Since this is such incredibly wonderful news, we have to get away from celebrating this sacrament as if it were a memorial service. So often on Communion Sundays in our churches it looks as if our Savior never rose from the grave. The elders are dressed in black, the organ plays dirges, the elements are covered with a large white sheet (which sure makes it look like there is a dead body under there). Then, worst of all, a minister may charge the congregation to sit silently in the pews and think about all the ways we are responsible for Jesus' death. Do any of us doubt it? I don't think so. What we are confused about, however, is how to find grace. *That* is why we are given this Table.

When we experience gracious communion with the risen Christ, it changes us. Thus, while the Reformed tradition has long asserted that the elements do not change at this Table, in recent years we have not adequately asserted that the communicants do change. This is how we continue to experience conversion: we are led by the Spirit to suffer with Christ at the Table, that we may also be glorified with him.

The old Pietists used a term that I have not heard in years—"mortification." Mortification is not the same as masochism, which delights in personal suffering, or even the same as asceticism, which turns away from bodily appetites. Mortification means killing off the parts of our lives that cannot stand before God. Thus, we die to the old, that we might live in Christ. But even this is too much for us to accomplish. Nothing is as enslaving as trying to change our lives. So we do not change in order to come to the Table. It is futile to try to make the Lord's Supper be about my self-righteousness. We are changed as a result of being at the Table. Paul makes it clear that it is only as we are led by the Spirit that we start to discover true change.

When I was seven years old, my father, who was a pastor, brought home a twelve-year-old boy named Roger. Roger was the only child of two drug addicts. My Dad had done all he could to intervene, but after years of sucking the life out of their little family to get drugs, the parents eventually killed themselves in a drug overdose. There were no other family members to take care of Roger, so my father brought him home, where he lived with us until he left home after high school to join the army.

As you can imagine, there was a big difference between our home and the one in which Roger grew up. With both parents typically stoned, Roger spent the first twelve years of life fending for himself. He was always scared there would not be a meal. He was frightened of adults and frightened of life itself. In Roger's earlier world, young and old were on their own. That's the logical extreme of our society that is so bent on always making it about you. So Roger was in for a big change at the church manse.

Most of the lessons Roger learned, it seemed, occurred at the table. So many times I heard my parents say, "No, no, Roger, that's not how we act here." It was hard work being in our family, and Roger had to learn a lot about sharing, manners, and chores. But did any of that hard work get Roger in the family? No; he was made part of the family by the grace of my father, who brought him home. *Sola gratia.* By grace he became my joint heir. Did he have to do a lot of work once he arrived? Oh, you bet he did. But it wasn't his effort that brought about the change in his life, it was the love of my parents. He was so overwhelmed by the grace he received that the changes he made came about from sheer gratitude.

Then a military announcement came telling us that Roger had been killed in an act of heroism in Vietnam. I remember my mother's tears most of all. She cried not only out of grief, but also out of thanksgiving that Roger had discovered how to believe in something other than himself. I like to think that it was the lessons of love he learned at the table that made the difference.

How about you? As the Spirit leads you to the Table, what is it that needs to be sacrificed, mortified? Like Roger, you have lived for a long time in a frightening world. So you have developed more than one life-draining skill to take care of yourself—anger and fear, hurt and cynicism, comfortable despair. Yet the Holy Spirit will never let you say that is who you are. No, that is not you! You are who God made you, and God did not make you angry or fearful or cynical or despairing. But you will never get rid of the ungodly part of life by trying hard. It is only as the Spirit leads you home to your place at this Table that you will be overwhelmed by the passion of a God dying to love you. Then you will discover you are taking on the very image of Christ, your joint heir.

That is the reality occurring here. There is no question of that. The question is, do you see it? Do you? Our world is quite literally dying for the church to give itself away. This Table is where the Spirit shows us how to do that.

Amen.

Doves, Deserts, and Bathtubs

Linda C. Loving

Then Jesus came from Galilee to John at the Jordan, to be bap-
tized by him. John would have prevented him, saying, "I need
to be baptized by you, and do you come to me?" But Jesus
answered him, "Let it be so now; for it is proper for us in this
way to fulfill all righteousness." Then he consented. And when
Jesus had been baptized, just as he came up from the water, sud-
denly the heavens were opened to him and he saw the Spirit of
God descending like a dove and alighting on him. And a voice
from heaven said, "This is my Son, the Beloved, with whom I
am well pleased."

Matthew 3:13–17

Whenever Kevin Costner does a baseball movie, it borders on a religious experience for me—in part because I find certain mystical qual-
ities in the game of baseball; in part because, well, Kevin Costner is
Kevin Costner. His most recent film, *For Love of the Game,* left me
with a powerful image that helps me to articulate a dimension of the
Holy Spirit. Now I want to be careful here to distinguish between
Hollywood and the Holy Spirit, though the boundaries do blur occasionally. Sometimes, in spite of ourselves, what we do in worship is

driven by a perceived need to entertain; sometimes, in spite of itself, what Hollywood does to entertain leads us to an encounter with the Spirit.

James Wahl of the *Christian Century*, with decades of experience critiquing films nationally and internationally, once told me that grace occurs in a film at the point where the director's life and the actor's life and the viewer's life intersect. Director-actor-viewer. That convergence is a moment of unpredictable grace when it happens, and obviously there are different intersections, creating different "graced moments" for different viewers. (Not unlike sermons—which can leave the preacher so baffled if Sunday morning feedback is taken too seriously!)

The moment of grace for me in the film *For Love of the Game* came when Costner stands on the pitcher's mound and tries to focus on the task at hand. You see in his face the pressure he feels, you hear the roar of distractions from the crowd, the coaches, the cries of teammates and vendors. You see this lone figure on the mound, potentially swallowed up by a stadium of sound, and then the pitcher's discipline kicks in. (I saw it as a spiritual discipline . . . really!) He stares at the plate and says to himself these three curious words: "Clear the mechanism." Clear the mechanism—a kind of mantra; a kind of prayer.

And with those words, the cacophony fades, almost as if a mute button had been hit, or as if a transparent sound screen had descended between the pitcher and the public. The voices—the cheers and jeers, compliments and curses—are no longer distinguishable, just a gentle background hum. His focus is utterly on the internal voice—the voice offering guidance, discipline, and strength . . . the voice offering the truth of that one moment, the accuracy of that one pitch, the confidence of knowing who you are and what you are to do and be. Everything else fades. "Clear the mechanism." Or, in my graced translation: Come, Holy Spirit, come. Clear the mechanism.

I wonder if that's what it was like for Jesus that day in the Jordan River. Did the dove's descent bring a holy moment when the cacophony of the crowd went to mute and Jesus accepted the embrace of the Holy Spirit and truly heard the truth of who he was and what he needed to do? Fluttering dove's wings shielding out the distractions of others' expectations, so that God's voice alone is heard, and there is a convergence that allows self-understanding—ultimate self-understanding. Bottom of the ninth self-understanding. "This is my Son, the Beloved, with whom I am well pleased." Clear the mechanism. Maybe that's what that dove is all about—Come, Holy Spirit, come—so that we may truly focus, truly hear who we are in God's sight, and thereby rise above all the other voices in our lives.

Clear the mechanism. Clear the decks. Clear our hearts and minds of the clutter. Clear out the temptations, the obsessions, the regrets, the blame. Clear out the clamor of culture so that we can truly receive the Spirit of God. Is that what that dove was doing???

Jesus himself needed to rise above the voices that would have distracted and detracted from his ultimate truth of being. Those voices followed quickly after his baptism as he was taken into the wilderness (and for all we know such voices may have preceded his baptism as well). We all struggle with voices of some kind—voices that need to be feathered out, as if by dove's wings, in order that we might know God's peace and truth.

The medieval mystic and spiritual guide Julian of Norwich, who wrote extensively of the Holy Spirit, struggled with voices in a very real way—voices not of God's Spirit, voices that distracted and destroyed. This is beautifully described in the play *Julian,* written by Jesuit priest J. Janda. Julian's version of "clear the mechanism" comes at a pivotal moment in the play, and, indeed, in her life. Let me share this excerpt from *Julian* with you.

> I suffered from noise, voices in my head. Often I could not sleep. Accusing voices endlessly telling me that I was responsible for all the evil and suffering in England. At times I could not hear myself nor any one else. It was as if I was judge, jury, attorney and condemned. I could not defend my helpless self. There were none to defend me. And I began to hate myself. The accusing, condemning voices grew louder and louder till I cried out to God that he in his mercy would give me peace—to live, to stop the voices! God heard my cries. The madness ended. The voices gave way to silence. For I was shown the suffering Christ, the forgiving Christ, and that has made the difference. It was an understanding . . . a deep understanding. How do I find words to tell of it? And with the understanding I could acknowledge my fear, my terror, my anger, my helplessness, my ignorance, my

> confusion. It was as if I could forgive myself and every
> other, for I felt in my heart God had forgiven me. I
> could now stop my self-hating, my blaming, and turn
> my life to simple tasks that make for peace—my own
> and others', and see for the first time the good in all and
> see God in all.[1]

Julian, like Jesus, spends significant time dealing with voices in the wilderness before she finds the truth of who she is and is able then to minister to others.

There are certainly more recent examples as well. A newly published biography of Jane Addams[2] (the founder of Hull House and a heroine in the field of social work) is a riveting reminder of the voices a woman of the Victorian age would need to overcome to hear such a call. Addams suffered depression as a girl and young woman as a result of all the voices of culture putting her down and holding her back. Stop the voices. Clear the mechanism. Come, Holy Spirit, come. And what a ministry of justice came forth against all odds!

A more recent inspiration is Martin Luther King Jr. He may be closer to us chronologically, but it seems we are no closer to understanding what wilderness voices he truly experienced. As I serve an urban church in the heart of Oakland, I learn day by day how much more I have to learn about the voices of racism. Joan Chittister, a Benedictine sister, writes this about King: "He struggled constantly with a feeling of inadequacy, a too-young awareness of death, pressures from the black community, and hysterical hostility from whites. . . . He was stabbed three times, physically attacked three more times, bombed in his home three times, and jailed fourteen times before he was shot to death."[3] Stop the voices. Clear the mechanism. Come, Holy Spirit, come. Chittister continues:

> King followed a light, saw a star, felt a pulse, was con-
> sumed by a vision that few of us ever see. He may have
> had to grapple with his own inner discipline, but he was
> deeply and consistently converted from the way things
> are to the ways of the will of God for us, and, in his con-
> centration on the things of God, he converted us all.
> Though angry, he was also committed to nonviolence.
> Though depressed, he was also awash in hope. Though
> struggling with the pressures of sensuality, he was also
> loving beyond measure.[4]

Clear the mechanism. Come, Holy Spirit. Come like a dove and feather out all that is not of God. Grant us focus, show us the truth of who we are and the tasks that are ours to do.

Jesus, Julian, Jane, Martin, you, me—one by one—seeking to hear the voice instilled in us from the beginning of time and sealed on our hearts at baptism. And the Presbyterian Church (U.S.A.), by grace, seeking to clear the mechanism, to stop the voices, to receive the Spirit. *Receive* the Spirit, not dictate the Spirit, not script the Spirit—receive the winged truth of each baptism.

In a way, baptism is a symbolic clearing of the voices. "This is my beloved child. You are my beloved child." The only voice that really matters; the only voice that will call us into true ministry.

Last December, at a dinner party in my home, I discovered two-year-old Lindsey unattended in my living room taking the olive wood figures of my precious nativity set purchased in Bethlehem and plunging them headfirst into the water in my floating candleholder. She was doing this boldly, unabashedly, water on the coffee table, the carpet, drenching the figures. She looked at me calmly and said she was "bathtubbing" them, like in church. Ah, yes, bathtubbing them. At times I think we could all stand to be plunged headfirst in cold water—to find our way again to the Spirit sealed on our hearts, to reclaim that new reality, that fundamental identity; to clear our heads, distracted as we are in the church by voices—voices of competition, self-righteousness, perfectionism, and power, voices of fear, prejudice, and judgment.

Clear the mechanism, dear God. Stop the voices—so that we may hear Yours alone. May the brush of dove's wings feather out all that distracts or divides or even demonizes us as individuals and as a church.

Theology professor Ben Reist of San Francisco Theological Seminary is known by students for claiming that the only thing harder to describe than the Trinity is the balk rule in baseball. Well, I can't believe I am at a national conference preaching on both at the same time! So let me just say that this sermon attempts to point to the Holy Spirit, but can neither define nor fully contain it—perhaps as the baseball diamond structures the game but does not contain it when you hit one out of the park (there is the reminder of infinity). In the meantime, there are these measured bases to run. In our blessed, baptized, forgiven lives, the Holy Spirit feathers in with an occasional pure moment in which we look up to see the ball soar out of the confinement of our innings—and there is a knowing, a voice, a perspective, the brush of wings, the spirited words, "You are my beloved. With you I am well pleased."

Clear the mechanism. Come, Holy Spirit, come. Amen.

NOTES

1. J. Janda, *Julian* (New York: Seabury Press, 1984), pp. 42–44.
2. Gloria Diliberto, *A Useful Woman: The Early Life of Jane Addams* (New York: Charles Scribner's Sons, 1999).
3. Joan Chittister, *Passion for Life* (Maryknoll, N. Y.: Orbis Books, 1996), p. 42.
4. Ibid., p. 39.

God-Breath

Nancy Copeland-Payton

The hand of the LORD came upon me, and he brought me out by the spirit of the LORD and set me down in the middle of a valley; it was full of bones. He led me all around them; there were very many lying in the valley, and they were very dry. He said to me, "Mortal, can these bones live?" I answered, "O Lord GOD, you know." Then he said to me, "Prophesy to these bones, and say to them: O dry bones, hear the word of the LORD. Thus says the Lord GOD to these bones: I will cause breath to enter you, and you shall live. I will lay sinews on you, and will cause flesh to come upon you, and cover you with skin, and put breath in you, and you shall live; and you shall know that I am the LORD."

So I prophesied as I had been commanded; and as I prophesied, suddenly there was a noise, a rattling, and the bones came together, bone to its bone. I looked, and there were sinews on them, and flesh had come upon them, and skin had covered them; but there was no breath in them. Then he said to me, "Prophesy to the breath, prophesy, mortal, and say to the breath: Thus says the Lord GOD: Come from the four winds, O breath, and breathe upon these slain, that they may live." I prophesied as he commanded me, and the breath came into them, and they lived, and stood on their feet, a vast multitude.

Then he said to me, "Mortal, these bones are the whole house of Israel. They say, 'Our bones are dried up, and our hope is lost; we are cut off completely.' Therefore prophesy, and say to them, Thus says the Lord GOD: I am going to open your graves, and bring you up from your graves, O my people; and I will bring you back to the land of Israel. And you shall know that I am the LORD, when I open your graves, and bring you up from your graves, O my people. I will put my spirit within you, and you shall live, and I will place you on your own soil; then you shall know that I, the LORD, have spoken and will act," says the LORD.
Ezekiel 37:1–14

"O Lord, hear my prayer," she whispers. "O holy God of Israel, why do you stand so far off? Why do you hide yourself in times of trouble?"

A soldier rudely shoves her. "Move on," he barks.

Clinging to the Temple courtyard wall, she breathes out, "My God, my God, why have you forsaken me? Why are you so far from saving me, so far from the words of my groaning?"

"Didn't you hear me?" he said. "Get moving."

He pushes her away from the Temple and into the chaos of Jerusalem streets.

Soldiers from Babylon shout orders. Babies scream, children clutch parents in terror, adults with bellies full of fear throw treasures of a lifetime on pack animals' backs.

"Come on, move. We don't have all day."

Babylon has captured Jerusalem. Rough soldiers push Ezekiel and his people out the northern gates of the city. The ragtag column of children and adults, babies and animals, scatter north for miles through the hills. Ezekiel the priest risks stopping to look back. King Solomon's Temple rises above city walls. As long as his people spew out the northern gates, they're still connected to the Temple, to the ark, to God's sacred promise of this land. But soldiers finally rout the last exiles out the gates . . . and the connection is broken.

Walking into exile, Ezekiel's prayer joins the woman's prayer. "How long, O Lord? Will you forget me forever? How long, O Lord? Will you hide yourself forever?"

Nine hundred miles; Ezekiel and his people walk nine hundred miles to Babylon, up and around the edge of the great Syrian wilderness. Their footsteps follow the ancient caravan route, with life-giving rivers always on their left and a dry desert of certain death always on their right. Syrian desert wind stings faces and burns nostrils. Tears fall on ground so dry it is devoid of all life.

Where . . . is God?

An anguished voice comes over the ambulance request line to me as a physician in the emergency room. "Come. Please hurry. My baby's not breathing." After forty-five minutes of unsuccessful resuscitation attempts, I leave the trauma room to tell the father his son is dead. He knows, deep inside, what I'm going to say as I enter the room. Not wanting to hear it, hoping against the odds his child is alive, he looks at me with a belly full of fear. Closing the door, sitting by him, taking his hand, I tell him everything that has happened. There's silence, then tears. His cries are anguished. Later I stay with him as he rocks the body of his baby. Sobbing uncontrollably, his grief is overwhelming.

Separated only by the veil of years, his prayer rises up with those of Ezekiel and his people.

"O Lord, hear my prayer. Save me, for the waters have come up to my neck. I sink in the miry depths where there is no foothold."

He walks home that night without his baby. He faces next morning's dawn in an empty house, where dry desert winds of certain death had howled through the night.

Where . . . is God?

They come to Constantinople. The people who will pen that part of the Nicaean creed come to Constantinople, polyglot city—it's said all seventy-two tongues of humankind are spoken here. Constantinople, where prayers from the great church Hagia Sophia rise heavenward. Constantinople, where Roman bureaucrats, builders of "oh, so straight roads" tying the empire together now meet twisting maze of Byzantine bazaar, where the path is choked by overflowing bags of fragrant spices, gleaming brass, intricate silk carpets. They come to Constantinople, about one hundred eighty-six men—yes, they're all men. What do you expect? It's the year 381. They come from the Eastern churches. It will be two hundred years before men of the Western

Church have their say in this creed, adding a clause that will further divide East and West.

The question that draws them to Constantinople? "Where is God?" Oh, it isn't the lament rising from the breaking of Ezekiel's people's hearts as they left Jerusalem for exile in Babylon. It isn't the tortured cry from a father's soul being ripped open.

But, it is the same question: "Where is God?"

They'd last met to struggle with the question in Nicaea. But that meeting and creed left unfinished business that bubbled under the surface, erupting in furious disputes. Arius, Athanasius bounced in and out of favor like Ping-Pong balls. Greed, political ambition, regional fighting—all mixed into the question. Emperors and bishops used Arianism as a stepping-stone to power. At a gathering in Milan, Arian bishops became so enraged they ripped the pen from the hand of the bishop of Milan as he was signing the creed from Nicaea. There was a riot. And these were the clergy, my friends. We won't even talk about the emperors.

Where is God?

Walking from Jerusalem into exile, walking from the ER into an empty house, seduced by power in Constantinople—we all journey through life skirting the edge of the wilderness. The desert is always on our right, so close its dry wind stings our faces and burns our nostrils. When we look into the certain death of the desert—we ask the wrong question.

Where is God?

God isn't lost.

The question is, "Where are we?"

Ezekiel tells us he and his people are in a desolate valley littered with sun-bleached, human bones. There's no sound. Eerie silence blankets this valley. Back and forth, Ezekiel's led through bones. Stepping over-around-upon them, the bones are so brittle they snap and break if he stumbles. He aches for a sign of life. But there isn't even a smell of death here; it has been so long since there was life, even the stench of decaying flesh is absent. In this vacuum without life, the air is so dry it hurts to breathe.

The father's nighttime walk from the ER into an empty house is a journey into Ezekiel's valley. Baby pictures on the mantel, bright infant toys scattered on the floor, an empty crib; he steps over-around-upon the remains of broken hopes for the future, once full of promise, now lifeless and so brittle they snap and break like the rattle he stumbles on.

Years before, the clergymen walking into Constantinople had felt intense stirrings of a call from God. They each answered the call, with fear and trembling that arose from deep within their soul. They once felt the weight of hands on them at ordination. Now they walk into Constantinople, ensnared in political power and ambition. Their gathering is littered with the dry bones of their long-ago answering of God's call. Their long-ago vows of humble and obedient service are so brittle they snap and break in Byzantine streets.

Ezekiel's valley—how many of us have walked there, stumbling over lifeless remains of relationships we have broken, mourning the death of those we love, burying the losses of a lifetime? How many of us have inhaled air so dry it hurts to breath?

The valley of bones. If we look in the dust of the valley floor, there are many footprints. Others have been this way before. If we listen in the silence, we hear the cry of those who passed this way just last year. If we listen hard, the crying grows louder, adding more and more voices as we listen back through the centuries. Finally we hear the ancient, soul-wrenching cry of Ezekiel's people: "Our bones are dried up, and our hope is lost; we are cut off completely."

But listen again. In Ezekiel's valley, with the cry of human lament through the ages, is something else. "I will cause breath to enter you, and you shall live." From the four winds, God-breath comes blowing free, surprising and unbounded. God-breath blows through an exiled people in Babylon, through a father's empty nursery, touching and healing the broken places in our lives where we hurt so deeply. God-breath blows through greed and ambition in Constantinople, inspiring words that speak to the depths of our souls, "We believe in the Holy Spirit, the Lord, the giver of life."

The Spirit breathes us into life in times of joy, that we may live more abundantly. The Spirit breathes us into life in anguish of despair, that we may live to get through the day. God-breath blows through sanctuary and kitchen, amidst stained-glass windows and broken glass of ghetto street. God-breath blows through Israeli and Palestinian firefighters battling a blaze side by side. God-breath blows in daffodil yellow pushing through winter snow, in a child's laugh and a senior's beaming smile.

God-breath flutters empty grave cloths that lie limp on a tomb's floor. God-breath hovers over the deep before each moment of creation and stirs the waters of baptism. God-breath leavens Communion bread, ferments Eucharist wine, and blows through our hair as we walk to Emmaus.

And God-breath blows through this place, in this hour; breathing life, glorious life, the "sun rising out of darkest night" kind of life, into all those places deep inside us we thought were dead.

God isn't lost . . . and neither are we.

Who Has the Spirit?

Gregory M. Busby

Then afterward
*   I will pour out my spirit on all flesh;*
your sons and your daughters shall prophesy,
*   your old men shall dream dreams,*
*   and your young men shall see visions.*
Even on the male and female slaves,
*   in those days, I will pour out my spirit.*

I will show portents in the heavens and on the earth, blood and
fire and columns of smoke. The sun shall be turned to darkness,
and the moon to blood, before the great and terrible day of the
LORD comes. Then everyone who calls on the name of the LORD
shall be saved; for in Mount Zion and in Jerusalem there shall
be those who escape, as the LORD has said, and among the sur-
vivors shall be those whom the LORD calls.

Joel 2:28–32

"Who has the Spirit?"

It seems like a hundred years ago that I was in high school. I can't remember all the classes I took, and I couldn't tell you the names of my teachers. But one thing I do recall from my days in high school is the cheerleaders.

There's more to my memories of those cheerleaders than the fact that they were easy on the eyes. One thing I remember well is the fancy routines these sisters had for all their cheers. They had all kinds of choreographed hand claps, and their fast and fancy footwork would have put Gregory Hines to shame. There's no doubt in my mind that if ESPN had been around in those days, our high school cheerleading squad would have won each year's national competition with no problems whatsoever!

As I think about our high school's cheerleading squad, I can't help but compare them to the cheerleaders we had in college. The college cheerleaders weren't as rhythmical as the ones I had known back home, and their routines weren't as precisely choreographed or polished. As I recall, their voices sounded more like the brothers in my church's Imani choir bass section than the high-voiced sisters who sing soprano for us. But even with stiffer routines and much deeper voices, one of their cheers still sticks in my mind after all these years. Whenever our football or basketball games seemed to be hitting a dry spot, our cheerleaders would look into the stands, put their hands to their faces, and yell out, "We've got spirit, yes we do! We've got spirit, how about you?"

And as those of us in the stands joined in yelling that cheer across the field to the other team's fans, their side would yell back the same cheer: "We've got spirit, yes we do! We've got spirit, how about you?" Then the two sides would take turns giving the cheer back, hopefully louder than the challenge that came across to them. On and on it would go, until one side felt it had gotten the better of the other in this spirited shouting match.

I guess I still keep these memories of those cheerleading squads from my past because in so many ways that old cheer reminds me so much of the Christian church that we're part of these days. We're all born-again, Bible-trusting believers in the Lord Jesus Christ and all that goes along with that, aren't we? But when it comes to talking about the Holy Spirit, our Christian-speak sounds more garbled than all those tongues that started wagging at Babel! We Presbyterians are part of God's church—the solid rock that Peter confessed, the body of believers for whom Christ bled and died—but we sound more and more like timid cheerleaders hesitantly calling out, "We've got the Spirit, yes we do. . . ." Those of us in the Presbyterian family are familiar with the Holy Spirit's name, and we know the Spirit as the bona fide third Person of the Holy Trinity. But when it comes to walking and talking about the Holy Spirit with any degree of familiarity, can we shout, "We've got Spirit, yes we do!" with conviction ringing in our voices?

Pentecostals, charismatics, and other Christian believers affirm the gifts of our Lord's Spirit on a regular basis. Yet, with their familiarity comes the danger of a tendency toward exclusivity. Some of them say that if you don't speak in tongues, offering up words of prophecy and knowledge when you praise the Lord, then your Christianity isn't all it could be. They don't break out the pompons as if it's a pep rally, but their sense of monopoly on Holy Spirit ownership sounds like a religious version of "We've got spirit, yes we do! We've got spirit, how about you?" all over again.

Lest you think I've gone from preaching to denomination-bashing, let me hasten to make a plea of not guilty as charged. It's not just Pentecostals and Presbyterians who sit at the polar opposites of this Holy Spirit spectrum. All across the Christian church there are all types of believers with different feelings on where the Holy Spirit fits into their lives. There are believers who sense the Spirit's presence when in high-praise worship with every instrument under the sun going full blast. Other Christians are most in touch with the Spirit when there's a still, small quietness all around them. Still others sense the presence of the Holy Spirit when they're working around the church, extending the love of Jesus with their hands. And then, there are those in the body of Christ who know they've had an experience of the Holy Spirit when the word of God has been shared, lives have been committed to Christ, and individuals have been changed for the better. All of us—members of one faith, one Lord, and one baptism—have so many interpretations and attitudes about who the Holy Spirit is and where that divine Spirit fits into our lives.

And so, as we've gathered for our convocation on a rain-soaked night in the heart of Charlotte, North Carolina, the question needs to be raised, "Who has the Spirit?" Is the Holy Spirit easy to obtain, or something that we've got to strive for? And how do we know when we're in the presence of the Lord's Holy Spirit when he shows up?

It's hard to say who has the Holy Spirit when our churches are too silent on some issues and too vocal on others. It's hard to get a handle on the Holy Spirit when so much is done in the name of God for political and personal purposes in this country. And it's especially hard to say for sure who has the Holy Spirit among us when our church's governing bodies seem more like holy terrors than earthly houses for the Holy of Holies!

We could commission a study team, contact the Gallup poll or some other organization, to get an answer on the subject. Yet, the timeless truths of Holy Scripture have answers for us that are more reliable than those of any focus groups we could measure by today's standards.

For almost eight hundred and fifty years before the birth of our Lord and Savior Jesus Christ, the Bible talks about an equally topsy-turvy time in the history of the world. Among the people of Judah, political upheavals were the order of the day. False religions were popping up all over the place, like uncontrollable weeds. God's chosen people were falling prey to these newfangled faiths like sheep being led to the slaughter. The corruption of kings was only exceeded by the corruption of the kingdoms they presided over. Morals and values were virtually nonexistent. The rich were getting richer, while the poor were practically invisible as far as the larger society was concerned.

Against this deplorable social backdrop, God raised up a prophet named Joel, a man whose only biographical detail is that he was the son of a guy named Pethuel. In this rather short book of the Old Testament, we see that while this obscure prophet dealt with a declining social fabric much like ours, he voiced a message of hope as well as judgment. Joel was the bearer of God's bad tidings, but he was also a beacon pointing toward better days for the people of Judah. He doesn't mince words about the calamities that are coming to God's people: a plague of locusts that will cover their land, wiping out their crops; an invading army from the north that will surround them on every side, spreading pain and suffering far and wide.

But just when it seems as if the message couldn't be any worse, Joel says that the Lord God will send out an olive branch toward God's people. As God's people turn back to God with a spirit of national repentance, the Lord God promises to restore their land and repel the

attacking army at the border. Then the prophet Joel brings a word
from the Lord with a promise for God's people:

> Then afterward
>   I will pour out my spirit on all flesh;
> your sons and your daughters shall prophesy,
>   your old men shall dream dreams,
>   and your young men shall see visions.
> Even on the male and female slaves,
>   in those days I will pour out my spirit.

Joel saw difficult days ahead for God's people in Judah, but as God's
prophet Joel could see another picture beyond his horizon—a time of
turning back to the Lord our God with a renewed sense of purpose
for being God's people.

In his day and time, Joel could never imagine a Christian church
with believers on every continent of the planet. I doubt if his mind
could have conceived Web sites, women in ministry, shared Commu-
nions, or even a messiah called Jesus. But what Joel *could* see still has
an air of relevance for the facing of this hour—a litmus test, if you
will, for where and on whom the Spirit rests.

Joel saw a time when the Lord's Holy Spirit would be poured out
on all flesh . . . a time when all humanity would be partakers of this
outpouring of God's grace. All of humanity . . . so it's a promise that
includes us in the Presbyterian Church (U.S.A.) as well! That's some
good news for us. So often we've seen ourselves as those fellows who
were driving a dairy truck on a hot summer day saw us. They were
making their daily deliveries when one of the tires blew out on the
back end of their truck. After spending some time wondering what
they could do to keep everything from spoiling or melting, one of the
men looked around and said, "I know! Let's put it in the Presbyterian
church across the way. It's so cold in there the ice cream will keep until
Labor Day." The perception of Presbyterians as "God's frozen chosen"
has been more the rule than the exception. But lest you think I came
to do some Presby-bashing this evening, I'm glad to say that old
stereotype is becoming a thing of the past.

"We've got the Spirit" in the PCUSA, as our worship together here
has so ably demonstrated. There was a time when gospel choirs like
our Imani Choir from First United were about as rare in our churches

as the Hope diamond. But, as the Lord continues to pour out his Spirit, we see more and more expressions of musical diversity like this popping up in congregations all across our denomination. Still, signs of the Holy Spirit's work go far beyond new and creative forms of worship and praise.

There are signs of the Holy Spirit at work here in the Presbytery of Charlotte. Our host for this conference, First Presbyterian, as well as First United are both doing noontime outreach worship services to the working population of our downtown's center. Memorial Church has broken new ground in Christian education with its "Wonderful Wednesdays" program, bringing the Sunday school experience to a day and time when the whole family can study the scriptures, while taking care of suppertime and homework needs as well. Newell Presbyterian Church is just one of many of our churches that have embraced their communities with a "Mother's Morning Out" experience, a time-out for moms that lends a hand to primary caregivers. I could go on and on naming similar signs of our Savior's Spirit in so many of our churches here in Charlotte . . . and, I'm sure, in your presbyteries and all across the nation.

But as Joel saw a day when the Lord's Spirit would be poured out on all flesh, aren't you glad to be a Presbyterian living in this century? While others are debating the question of ordaining women as elders and ministers, aren't you glad to know that we affirmed that move of the Holy Spirit a half century ago? The church of Jesus Christ has certainly been much better for it! It's a question the Holy Spirit hasn't finished putting before us as we wrestle with the question of ordaining gay men and women to those same offices of the church. We go back and forth on both sides of this difficult issue, and yet, as we disagree, I thank God that we're learning how to disagree in love, instead of in angry words and actions toward one another. Nothing less than the Holy Spirit of our Savior could accomplish that among us.

And the Holy Spirit allows us to continue being "the church reformed and always being reformed." We continue to seek justice in the world through new moves of the Spirit like the Hawkins-Buchanan Fund for Racial Justice, a move on the part of Presbyterians to seek reconciliation on the challenges of race as we move into a brand-new century.

So if someone asks, "Do you have the Spirit?" shout back, "Yes, we do!" We have the Spirit, my sisters and brothers of the Presbyterian Church (U.S.A.), because it's an outpouring promised to us by the authority of Holy Scripture. We've got the Spirit because the Spirit of our Lord is an inclusive, overflowing reality of God's presence with *all* God's people! We've got the Spirit as we dream new dreams! The Spirit is with us as we live out bolder visions for where our Savior wants our church to go.

And we shall always have this sweet heavenly dove staying right here with us as we continue preaching the love we've been filled with. The sweet communion of Christ's Spirit will linger as we're faithful in proclaiming the gospel's good news to a hurting world that is desperate for some healing. We can know we have the Holy Spirit leading and guiding us as we speak prophetically against all the principalities of sin and injustice as we've been called to—in season and out! And, without a doubt, we can be assured we have his Spirit as we lead others to call on that name that is above every name on earth for their salvation as a gift from God's grace.

"We've got the Spirit, yes we do," my sisters and brothers of the PCUSA. As we leave this place tonight, with hopes of returning tomorrow, may we leave understanding ourselves to be those latter-day sons and daughters about whom Joel prophesied so many years ago. May we walk in the newness of life that only a fresh outpouring of Christ's Holy Spirit can give. And may we take our places back in the world, knowing that come what may, his presence and the presence of that sweet Holy Spirit will go with us until the end of the age.

Praise God for his covenant promise, praise God from whom all eternal blessings flow. Amen.